LIVE AND LEARN

The Story of Denman College 1948-1969

LIVE AND LEARN

The Story of Denman College 1948-1969

BARBARA KAYE

NATIONAL FEDERATION OF WOMEN'S INSTITUTES

Published January 1970
by the
National Federation of Women's Institutes,
39 Eccleston Street, London, S.W.1

© NFWI 1970

SBN 900556 07 2

Set in Bembo twelve point on thirteen point and printed by
Novello & Company Ltd., Borough Green, Sevenoaks, Kent

CONTENTS

FOREWORD

by

Miss Sylvia M. Gray, M.B.E., Chairman, N.F.W.I.

The story of Denman College is the story of an idea that became a reality. This is often the story of many worthwhile projects but the fact that this idea germinated in the minds of a handful of W.I. members and has grown into a flourishing reality for nearly half a million gives it a special significance.

It was an idea that needed imagination, courage and tenacity if it was to be fulfilled and the members of today have cause to be grateful to those who fired the imagination of the members at the Annual Meeting in 1945 so that there and then they decided they would have a College of their own.

The following pages are a record of many things that have gone to make the College the place we know today. It tells of brilliant ideas, of mistakes and disappointments, and of achievement. Running through it all, however, can be discerned a thread of determination that it should be a place of quality – the house itself, the grounds, the furnishings and food bear witness to this. Quality in these practical things is important and easy to discern.

What is perhaps even more important but more difficult to define is the quality of thought, imagination and teaching that has given Denman such a special atmosphere.

Our thanks are due to countless W.I. members, staff and friends who over the years have given, so generously, money, time and thought that the College should grow from strength to strength.

As these words are being written the splendid new buildings are nearing completion. They will provide in a modern setting up-to-date equipment for the ever widening range of courses.

It will be that same spirit, however, of determination that we have quality in all things that will ensure the continued success of Denman College and the enrichment of the lives of the members who come there.

January 1970.

ACKNOWLEDGEMENTS

I am greatly indebted to the many W.I. members who have helped me with material for this book; in particular past and present members of the Denman College Committee.

I would also like to thank the staff of Denman College and of N.F.W.I. Headquarters, including former members of the staff, for their kindness and co-operation.

Finally, I would like to thank Mrs Craig, the W.I. member who did the typing.

BARBARA KAYE

COVER PHOTOGRAPHS

Front Page: The College as it is today; a painting course; car maintenance.

Back Page: Soil testing for archaeological remains; children on a course for members and families; part of the walled garden

CHAPTER I

Conference of Countrywomen

On a late September day in 1943 close on a hundred women set off from market towns and villages in many parts of England and Wales, to make their way to the town of Shrewsbury.

A few were young, a few elderly; mostly they were in their middle years. Some were farmers' wives, some had husbands in the Forces, some were the wives of business or professional men, some were single. One or two were school teachers or held some other professional job; one was a village postmistress. But if their backgrounds, ages and education varied widely they had one thing in common – they were all members of the Women's Institutes on their way to a residential conference on education and social security in post-war Britain, the first of its kind ever held by their National Federation.

Waiting to welcome them at Radbrook College was Mrs Adeline Vernon, who was to chair the conference; a quiet, determined woman, well-liked and respected by her fellow members. An ardent believer in the need for women to become better educated and better informed, the conference was, for her, a momentous occasion, the culmination of months of preparatory work; if her plans went right it was to be a milestone on the road to the fuller and wider education of countrywomen through the Women's Institutes.

With her were two members of the National Federation's Headquarters' staff, who had come on ahead to make the necessary arrangements. One was Miss Elizabeth Christmas, N.F.W.I. General Organizer, the other Miss Cecily McCall, Organizer to the Education Sub-committee, which was convening the conference. Both were young women, doing a job they believed in and enjoyed.

Since the beginning of the year Cecily McCall had spent much of her time travelling around the country on behalf of the Education Committee, arranging W.I. one-day schools on education and the planning of Britain's future Welfare State. These were intended to both inform and stimulate the members to take an active interest in such matters, and at the same time prepare the ground for the autumn conference.

In general the attendances had been pretty good; but it was one thing for a busy housewife to take a day off to attend a local conference, and quite another for her to leave home in war-time to spend four days on a concentrated course. So, not surprisingly, there had been some doubt as to whether more than a handful would come to Shrewsbury.

Radbrook, a domestic science college, run by Miss Bode and Miss Hutton, two liberal-minded women known for their enlightened views on education (debs and domestic servants studied cookery there together) was more comfortable than most educational establishments, and altogether an agreeable and suitable place for the conference. In any case, for most of those who attended, to be able to forget ration books, the cooker and the sink for four days and apply their minds to something completely different was sheer bliss.

On the morning after their arrival the first lecture was given by Clement Davies, a Liberal M.P. and an eloquent Welshman. His subject was the Beveridge Report, which had been published in 1942 and widely discussed ever since. After the lecture the conference split up into groups to discuss the various proposals in the Report – health insurance, maternity grants and so on. Later the students were delighted to learn that the notes taken on their discussion by the group leaders were being sent to Sir William Beveridge.

For its main speaker the conference had Sir Richard Livingstone, President of Corpus Christi College, Oxford, and an authority on adult education, who had chosen as the title for his talk "Education in a World Adrift".

Before the lecture Adeline Vernon and Cecily McCall took him aside. Would he, they asked, include in his speech the suggestion that the W.I's consider starting a college of their own?

This was an idea that had been in Adeline Vernon's mind for some time. An Oxford graduate herself, she wanted to see education – academic as well as practical – made available to ordinary countrywomen, as it was in the Scandinavian Folk Schools, and she believed this was something the W.I. could do. She had discussed her idea with a few like-minded fellow members who had warmly agreed with her, and had then decided that Sir Richard would be the ideal person to launch it; the conference the best possible place.

As she had expected, Sir Richard warmly approved and promised to do all he could to help.

He was always an inspiring speaker and on this occasion he was at his best. After speaking of the Danish Folk Schools he went on to a vigorous criticism of the British Government for having made no provision for adult education in the recent White Paper it had published (on which the 1944 Education Act was based) describing this as a "disgraceful omission" considering that "most of the electors of the next thirty years will have left school at the age of fourteen".

Finally he threw out a challenge, which must have made those not already in the know sit up in their chairs. "Why", he asked, "should not the Women's Institutes fill the gap? Why don't *you* start a people's college yourselves?"

When the lecture ended there was considerable excitement. Everyone was discussing the idea. Sir Richard's praise of the W.I. movement in general and of the recent W.I. questionnaire on education in particular had left his audience in a somewhat exalted mood, so that the feeling that the challenge must be taken up quickly became a conviction.

Adeline Vernon was well aware of the importance of striking while the iron was hot. An adroit campaigner, her plans had been made well in advance and she had already briefed one of the members to move a formal resolution that the W.I. should found a "People's College". Later in the day, when the conference was gathered to discuss Sir Richard's lecture, the proposition was put forward – and carried with great enthusiasm.

"The high spot of the conference was the idea Sir Richard left with us," reported Cecily McCall in *Home and Country* (the official W.I. magazine) the following month. "A Conference House where we could meet together for a day or longer . . . a hostel, holiday home (with nursery attached) and perhaps somewhere in the grounds a W.I. cottage built to the housewife's design for convenience and beauty.

"Just an outsize dream? Not if we want it enough. Then it might become a thrilling possibility."

CHAPTER II

Plans and Doubts

Soon after the Radbrook Conference Adeline Vernon attended the autumn Consultative Council – the twice yearly gathering of representatives from the county federations and members of the Executive at which future policy is discussed and resolutions selected for the A.G.M.

She had been asked by Lady Denman, the Chairman of the National Federation, to report on the conference, and this she did, telling the meeting that it had been a great success. Impressed by Mrs Vernon's account, a delegate from East Kent suggested that a similar conference should be held the following year; a suggestion that was later adopted. Meanwhile, those whose imagination had been fired by the idea of a W.I. college took advantage of the opportunity provided by the council meeting to spread the word and collect support.

Useful though it had been as a start for the campaign, the Radbrook Conference recommendation could not, by itself, set any wheels in motion. There was only one way in which that could be done; a resolution asking that a college be founded must be voted on to the agenda of the Annual General Meeting and adopted by a two-thirds majority of the delegates, voting on behalf of their institutes.

The first step, therefore, was to persuade either the National Executive, or one of the county federations, or – for that matter an institute – to draft a suitable resolution and submit it to the next Consultative Meeting at which the resolutions for the 1944 Annual General Meeting would be selected – always provided that this meeting could be held, for although there had been an Annual General Meeting in 1943 (attended by Her Majesty the Queen) it had not been possible to hold one in 1940, '41 or '42.

It could have been said that there was no great hurry, since even if the institutes voted for a college nothing could be done while the war was still being waged, but by the autumn of 1943 things were going a lot better on all fronts. Italy had capitulated and the Allied Forces were steadily advancing towards Rome. Germany was being pounded daily by our bombers; the tide had turned on the Russian front and against the Japanese in the Pacific. Most people believed that the following spring would see the Allies landing in France. The more optimistic talked of the war being over by Christmas 1944.

In any case, whether it was over in one year or two, there was a feeling that the time had come to raise one's eyes from the grey, ration-controlled present and fix them on what must, surely, be a brighter future. As had happened during the first world war many women had discovered in themselves capabilities that they had not known they possessed; they had organized and administered, often with outstanding success. When the war was over such women would want more than the narrow confines of an ordinary home. It was of women such as these, and of others whose talents were still latent, that the pioneers of the W.I. College project were thinking, as they made plans and enlisted support.

The Radbrook Conference had given them not only proof that there was a demand for adult education amongst W.I. members, but the go-ahead to cater for that demand, and they were certainly not going to put their plans into mothballs until the war ended.

Back at home after the Conference, the women who had been to Radbrook did what they could to arouse interest in the idea of a W.I. college in their own institutes, with varying success. In the northern counties a fairly usual reaction was that the college would almost certainly be situated in the south and therefore the distance would be too great for most members to have any benefit from it. Another argument against the college, often encountered, was that it would be better to concentrate on persuading local education authorities to provide more opportunities for adult education in the form of day or evening courses – as many already did.

Thirty-five counties had been represented at Radbrook so it was not long before the idea of a W.I. college was being discussed in all parts of the country, favourably or not, and as a fair proportion of the women who had attended belonged to the higher echelons of their county federations, they were in a position to press for action or, at least for support of any action that might be taken. Appropriately, the two counties which took up the idea with the greatest enthusiasm were Oxfordshire and Cambridgeshire.

When the spring Consultative Council was held, early in 1944, there was still no final decision as to whether there should be an Annual General Meeting in London that year. The "second front" was expected in the spring or summer and it was felt that there might be reprisals from the enemy; also if there were heavy casualties from the landings on the continent extra transport would be needed for the wounded, so that to bring hundreds of women to London by train might be thought irresponsible. In the event, the decision to postpone the meeting until the autumn was taken a few weeks later.

No actual resolution for a W.I. college was put forward at this meeting, but Mrs Hopkinson from Cambridgeshire had been briefed by her county to suggest that a W.I. Conference House should be established where residential courses could be held, and that the N.F.W.I. Executive Committee should "explore the idea". This proposal was welcomed by a large majority of the county representatives. Another suggestion that money might be raised to buy a "rest home" for members – or even two homes, one in the north and one in the south – found little response. Well-intentioned though this idea was, it was right off beam from the mood of the meeting, which was all for action and enterprise, rather than rest and recuperation.

When the Executive met in May, following the decision to postpone the A.G.M., the W.I. College proposal came up for discussion. Before this meeting Lady Denman had expressed some doubts about the idea: "Do you really think the members *want* a college?" she had wondered.

She was not the only one to have doubts. Other members of the Executive were dubious about the practicability of the project as well as whether the Movement could afford it. But the pro-college group which included, as well as Mrs Vernon, Mrs Esther Neville Smith, also an Oxford graduate, Lady Worsley-Taylor, a National Federation Vice-Chairman, and Lady Brunner, a newcomer to the Executive from Oxfordshire, were too enthusiastic and determined to be denied. Eventually they were instructed to go ahead and look into the idea.

Already they had done some preliminary research into educational institutions run by other voluntary organizations, such as Foxlease, the Girl Guide College, and they were currently trying to arrange a regular annual booking of accommodation for W.I. summer schools in one or other of the women's colleges in Oxford or Cambridge – though this finally came to nothing.

There was, in fact, nothing new in the W.I. running residential schools. Several of the counties had done so, and from as far back as 1919 potential leaders had been trained as Voluntary County Organizers (popularly known as V.C.O's) at residential courses.

In the early days such "schools" had often taken place in country houses, but as domestic staff became scarce so did willing hostesses, and other accommodation had had to be found. During the war this had become more and more of a problem, so that with the demand (proved by Radbrook) for more residential courses, where members could really get down to studying subjects or activities that interested them, a good case could be made out for the W.I. to have its own conference house.

CHAPTER III

The First Hurdle

"If you want to know what a W.I. college will be like you should have been at the 'Questions of the Day Course' held at Radbrook College in September", wrote Cecily McCall, reporting on the second N.F.W.I. educational conference, in *Home and Country*.

The theme this time was "The Home and the School". A psychologist from the Tavistock Clinic lectured on the "Parent and Child" and a professor from Bristol University on "Freedom from Want". Rather fewer students attended than the previous year, but those who went found it stimulating, instructive and friendly, and were eager for a similar conference the following year.

Because of the flying bombs that had begun to descend on London and the Home Counties that summer the A.G.M. had been cancelled, but plans were going ahead to hold the 1945 meeting in the spring or early summer, by which time, everyone hoped and prayed, the war would be over. Meanwhile the Oxfordshire Federation, urged on by Elizabeth Brunner, who was a member of the County Executive Committee, and by Miss Helena Deneke, a historian and fellow of Lady Margaret Hall, Oxford, who had been at the Radbrook Conference and knew Sir Richard well, decided to send a resolution to the next A.G.M.

It ran as follows: "That this meeting welcomes the suggestion of a Women's Institute College, notes with satisfaction the power to provide grants for such a purpose in Clause 100 of the Education Act 1944, and instructs the Executive Committee to make the necessary arrangements."

Anticipating opposition on the grounds of expense, the Oxfordshire members hoped to counter it by showing that the college could expect a grant from the Ministry of Education. It was just as well they could not know what a hard fight they would have before such help was forthcoming.

Elizabeth Brunner had, by this time, become one of the most enthusiastic of the small group who were actively working to promote the idea of a W.I. college. From the moment she had learnt of the project she had, in her own words, felt "on to an important thing". She saw it as a new and exciting challenge – just what the W.I. needed. It was largely due to her drive and determination to overcome all obstacles that the idea eventually became a reality.

She was, at this time, a comparatively new member and a good deal younger than most of the Executive. Born into a famous theatrical family, a daughter of Dorothea Baird and a grand-daughter of Henry Irving, she had been brought up in the theatre. Tall, slim and good-looking, it seemed natural that she should become an actress. By the time she was sixteen she was playing Titania in *A Midsummer Night's Dream* in the West End.

Other parts followed, but early in her twenties she had some trouble with her throat and decided to give up the stage. Marriage to Felix (later Sir Felix) Brunner and the arrival of four sons in fairly quick succession kept her too busy in the home for many outside interests, but when the family moved to Henley and her sons were at school, she joined the W.I. Quickly spotted as a potential leader, she was elected to the Oxfordshire Federation Executive Committee, then co-opted on to the National Federation's Education Sub-committee and a year later, in 1943, elected to the National Executive.

Such a swift ascent of the W.I. ladder was exceptional, but Lady Denman was a shrewd talent spotter and she had seen in Elizabeth Brunner the mixture of idealism, vision and drive that the Movement would need in the post-war years.

That the Oxfordshire resolution would be accepted for the 1945 A.G.M. was by no means a foregone conclusion, though most people thought it had a pretty good chance. It is usual for a large number of resolutions to be submitted, and because there had only been one Annual General Meeting held during the war (in 1943) there was naturally a big build-up, so, when the representatives of the county federations turned up at the January Consultative Council meeting to do their job of selection, they found themselves confronted by a list of well over a hundred resolutions, more than half dealing with public questions of one sort or another. From these they were expected to choose fourteen.

Fortunately the W.I. College resolution came early on the list, so the audience was still fresh when Miss Deneke, the Oxford representative, stood up to make the very brief speech allowed to sponsors of resolutions.

As an old friend of the late Grace Hadow, one of the pioneers of the W.I. Movement, and herself known and admired for her scholarship and her W.I. work, she was an excellent advocate for such a resolution. At this stage it was not a question of whether the Consultative Council and the Executive were themselves in favour of a W.I. College, but of whether or not the idea should be put to the institutes at the A.G.M.

For the county representatives, conscientiously listening to all the other sponsors of resolutions, it was a question of priority, as well as suitability. But when the long list had been reduced to a short list and the short list had been reconsidered, discussed and voted on, Oxfordshire's resolution was one of the lucky fourteen.

Now that this first hurdle had been overcome, Mrs Vernon, Elizabeth Brunner and other members of the Education Committee hoped that the National Executive might agree to give it their blessing when it came to be debated at the A.G.M. But Lady Denman was not in favour of this. It had always been her policy to "leave it to the institutes". If they wanted a W.I. College they would vote for one, without any prodding from the Executive. On the other hand, she suggested that if one of the institutes liked to put forward an amendment, asking that the Executive should get on with the job straight away, this might be helpful in strengthening the original resolution.

This suggestion was accepted; Elizabeth Brunner carried back the message to the Oxfordshire Executive, and Mrs Barbara King, a lively up-and-coming member of South Stoke W.I. agreed to propose the amendment on behalf of her institute who were all in favour of the college idea.

There were now some 6,000 Institutes in England and Wales, and close on 300,000 members. During March every institute received a copy of the agenda for the A.G.M. with the fourteen selected resolutions, which they were expected to discuss at their monthly meeting and brief their delegate on how to vote. Several were aimed at Government Departments; the Postmaster General was asked to improve the status of sub-postmasters, the Ministry of Housing to modernize rural cottages, the need for more village halls was urged, and so on. The members were used to debating resolutions of this sort, they had been doing it since the Women's Institutes first came into existence. However, the W.I. College resolution was a very different, not to say startling, proposition, and despite the articles in *Home and Country*, many members now learnt of the idea for the first time.

How would they vote? There were the cautious who thought the idea too grandiose and likely to prove far too expensive, the enthusiasts who thought it splendid, and the middle of the roaders, who didn't feel strongly one way or another and were quite happy to leave it to their delegate to vote whichever way she liked. These last were the amiable, tolerant majority who couldn't see themselves ever going to college, W.I. or any other, but wouldn't oppose the idea if other people thought it a good one. Thus, in many cases, the decision on how to vote was left to the discretion of the delegate after hearing the arguments, for and against, put forward at the Albert Hall – an arrangement frequently adopted by W.I's when they have difficulty in making up their collective mind.

CHAPTER IV

Put to the Vote

There is always a great sense of occasion as the Albert Hall fills with countrywomen, coming from every part of England and Wales to attend what has been called "the countrywoman's parliament". Timid delegates, pressed into representing their institute because "there's no one else who can go", discover a reassuring feeling of unity as they mingle with other delegates, crowding into the vestibule.

As they find their way up into "the gods", or downstairs into the arena, or wherever their county has been placed; as they pick out a familiar face here or there, gaze around the great, packed hall bright with gay hats and spring clothes; as they stand up to sing *Jerusalem*, their voices helping to swell a great volume of song, there is an exciting feeling of purpose, even of power.

Sitting on the platform with the other members of the Executive, holding her carefully prepared speech, Elizabeth Brunner waited with tight strung nerves for the moment when she must go to the microphone to move the W.I. College resolution on behalf of the Oxfordshire Federation. It was the last resolution to be taken before the luncheon break. Those that preceded it had produced some lively debates; some had been turned down.

This would be the first time she had spoken at the Albert Hall – a daunting experience for anyone, and to make matters worse she had a cold, but from her girlhood years in the theatre she knew that to suffer from nerves before the curtain goes up is no bad thing and often results in a heightened performance.

The Chairman caught her eye; the moment had come. As she got up to go to the microphone, a tall, youthful figure, slim and hatless, there was a sudden tautening of interest.

She was allowed eight minutes for her speech. She began with a reference to the Scandinavian folk schools, held up by Sir Richard

Livingstone and others as the best kind of example of after-school education for ordinary people, then she set herself to dispel the idea that a college must be bleak and institutional.

"I want you to imagine a place that will be homely and welcoming", she said, and went on to paint a picture of groups of women learning practical crafts, studying the arts and becoming better informed in the pleasantest possible surroundings away from the responsibilities and distractions which beset their normal lives.

Women would come from all parts of England, creating a richer, more diverse background than could be found at any local or regional college. There could be courses in handicrafts, horticulture, the domestic arts, in citizenship and world affairs; there would be relaxation and fun for women of all kinds and ages.

As she talked, the enthusiasm and the ring of conviction in her voice kindled an answering enthusiasm amongst her listeners. She had caught their imagination and throughout her speech, whether or not they all agreed with her, she held it.

She was brief on the financial aspects of the project. Some help would be sought from the Ministry of Education, but "W.I.'s in supporting the idea of a college of their own must expect to have some financial responsibility for the raising of funds". This was something of an understatement, but there was no point in frightening the delegates by mentioning the very large sums of money that would eventually be needed.

Still within her eight minutes she summed up: the college could be a much needed home and focus of the movement. It would attract younger members and open new vistas to older ones. As well as the teaching of everyday practical things there would be inspiration and a vision of wider horizons, so that life and the living of it became more worthwhile.

Cambridgeshire had asked that they should be allowed to second the resolution. Their representative, Mrs Hopkinson, was careful to make the point that her county had been in favour of the idea from the start and had already issued a pamphlet advocating a W.I. conference house. And why not a model nursery school attached to the college, where mothers could leave their children in safe care while taking courses!

It was then the turn of the opposition. Some had been briefed by county federations, others by their W.I's. Mrs Griffiths from a village in Warwickshire felt sure that wherever the college was built it would be inaccessible for some members, and was equally sure it would be better for the Institutes to co-operate with existing educational establishments for adult education.

Ironically, despite the Radbrook conferences, the Shropshire Federation also opposed the resolution. They were sure that the amount of money needed had been underestimated and they did not believe that any of the local authorities would give grants towards capital expenditure on the project. Another objection was that as so many members would find it difficult to leave their homes and children, the students would only be drawn from a section of the membership and would not be representative. This was a point that brought some applause.

Other delegates opposed the resolution on the grounds that it was not right to ask the ordinary member to raise money for something for which she would receive no benefit, and a member from East Kent declared: "The average countrywoman has neither the time nor the money to spare for long journeys; I think she can get all she needs from the county."

The college supporters now fired their second gun. Barbara King, who was to propose the amendment, had been well briefed by Elizabeth Brunner and Helena Deneke; she had also practised her speech in the corridor of the train on her way to London, when she had discovered, to her horror, that her feet, by this time growing colder and colder, were still encased in her gardening boots!

Terrified, but game, she reached the microphone somehow; heard Lady Denman murmur: "Be brief", found her voice and moved the amendment on behalf of South Stoke, that the words "instructs the Executive Committee to make the necessary arrangements", should be added to the resolution.

"Who knows", she cried, "the right house in the right place may be discovered at any moment. How grievous it would be if the Executive were not in a position to clinch the deal, or accept an offer!"

Speeches by supporters of the amendment from Staffordshire and Gloucestershire followed. "We do not want this college when we are all so old we have to be taken there in a bath chair!" said the Gloucestershire delegate emphatically. "We want it now."

At this point Lady Denman interposed a warning from the Chair.

"I do not want you to think that the college will be in existence when we meet next year," she remarked. She then put the amendment. At once a forest of voting cards shot up in all parts of the hall. There was no need to count them.

Before the amended and considerably strengthened resolution was put, it was right and proper that a senior member of the Executive should give it her blessing. This was ably done by Esther Neville Smith.

There were, as always, members who wanted to ask questions. Cards waved urgently here and there and distant voices, thinned by the poor acoustics, tried to be heard. With the expertise of long experience Lady Denman dealt crisply with each in turn.

"If the courses are only for two days, or a week, would they be any use?"

Lady Denman: "I think they would be."

"Would the college be non-political?"

Lady Denman: "I think the questioner means would it be non-party. It would certainly be non-party."

"How is it proposed to finance this college?"

Lady Denman: "Obviously the institutes would have to raise money . . . and we all know that the institutes are past-masters in the art."

Finally, after Elizabeth Brunner had returned to the microphone to answer some of the points raised, the question was put to the meeting. Once again the hands shot up, waving their red voting cards; once again there was no need to count them.

"That is carried," said Lady Denman. "So now we are pledged to a very important piece of work."

CHAPTER V

House Hunting

The day after the A.G.M. there was a N.F.W.I. Conference on Education in London. Its purpose was to discuss education in rural areas in the light of the 1944 Education Act, which appeared to hold out the promise of direct grants for such W.I. activities as the Handicraft and Produce Guilds, and other educational work including the W.I. College.

Elizabeth Brunner, fresh from what everyone agreed was a personal triumph in putting over the college resolution, was amongst the speakers. There was general rejoicing over the institutes' acceptance of the challenge, and a good deal of discussion on the courses that could be provided at the college and on their duration. Having sorted out its ideas on education in rural areas, and (although this was not in doubt in the minds of delegates) on the value of the W.Is' contribution in this field, the Conference agreed that a memorandum embodying these should be sent to the Ministry of Education.

Four weeks later a W.I. College Committee held its first meeting under the Chairmanship of the Hon. Mrs Methuen, a Wiltshire member who had just become Hon. Treasurer of the National Federation.

Like all good treasurers Grace Methuen was wary of open-ended financial commitments. Although she had not been out of sympathy with the idea of a W.I. College she had had some reservations on financial grounds, believing that those in favour of the project were optimistic in their estimates as to what it would cost. She had voted for the resolution, nevertheless: "It was not the sort of resolution one could vote against", she said later, and she was ready to do all she could to ensure that it was carried through successfully. Other members of the College Committee were Adeline Vernon, Esther Neville Smith, Elizabeth Brunner and Miss

Dora Tomkinson, a small but formidable woman, with a fiery temper who was at that time Chairman of the Agriculture Sub-committee.

By then Cecily McCall had resigned from her job as Education Organizer in order to stand as a Labour candidate in the General Election, but the help and advice of Frances Farrer, the N.F.W.I. General Secretary (later to become Dame Frances) was available to the committee.

At this preliminary meeting they decided they must concentrate on two primary tasks – finding a suitable house and finding the money not only to buy it, but also to furnish and maintain it. Everyone agreed that the bulk of the money would have to come from the institutes, meanwhile there were two sources they hoped to tap, the Carnegie United Kingdom Trust (which might look at them kindly since Lady Denman was one of the Trustees) and the Ministry of Education, where Mr R. A. Butler had given place to Miss Ellen Wilkinson.

The sort of house they had in mind was one large enough to sleep at least 25 students, plus a staff of nine or ten. It would have a hall that could be used for music and drama, rooms for handicraft demonstrations and two kitchens, one of which would be used for teaching domestic economy. There should also be a large vegetable garden both to provide the college with its own produce and allow students to take courses in horticulture.

These were practical points, but they wanted more than this. The college of their dreams would be a building of elegance – dignified, yet welcoming, set in spacious grounds and charming rural surroundings. It would be a house in which they themselves would be glad to live, and above all, comfortable.

As a first step to this end they appointed a small house-hunting sub-committee consisting of two senior members of the N.F.W.I. Executive, Mrs Vernon and Mrs Methuen, and Elizabeth Brunner. They then went off to attend a five-day residential school on "The Future of the Village" held, this time, at Somerville College, Oxford.

With the war in Europe over it seemed likely that some of the large houses that had been requisitioned by the Government, or taken over by industry, might soon be coming on the market. By the end of the summer this was already happening, and as a date for vacant possession could seldom be given prices were still fairly moderate.

Between July and September the three-woman sub-committee had heard of several houses through the good offices of the National Trust, but only one really appealed to them. This was "Wood Eaton", a beautiful eighteenth-century place in Oxfordshire. Unfortunately it was still occupied by a department of the B.B.C. who couldn't say when they might move out.

Apart from this there was a castle in Gloucestershire and two abbeys – Wroxton near Banbury, and Laycock in Wiltshire-but none turned out to be practical propositions.

When the main committee met again in September, Mrs Methuen, who had enough to do as the National Federation's honorary treasurer, preferred not to continue as chairman and Elizabeth Brunner was unanimously elected. This was an office she was to hold for the next six years. At the same time Miss Nancy Tennant, a Vice-Chairman of the National Federation, joined the committee.

Urgent as it was to find a house it was equally urgent to find the money to pay for it. Discreet sounding of the Carnegie United Kingdom Trust showed that the W.I. might hope for some help from that quarter; there was still no news of a grant from the Ministry, but as it was known that the Townswomen's Guilds had been promised a grant of £3,500 it seemed reasonable to think that Ellen Wilkinson would be equally, if not even more generous towards the W.Is.

That autumn, even though they still had no house in view, the committee worked out a provisional budget for running the college, reckoning that the students would pay somewhere between £2 and £3 a week for accommodation. Promises of help and money were already coming in from the institutes, although the appeal fund had not yet been launched. The Isle of Ely offered to furnish a room as a memorial to a member who had just died, and other county federations offered gifts of furniture.

Throughout the winter and spring of 1946 the hopes of the committee were often raised by reports of likely properties, but on inspection they all turned out to be unsatisfactory in one way or another. Wood Eaton remained the only house at all suitable for their purpose, and the B.B.C. were still in occupation.

It was a frustrating situation. Almost a year had gone by since the decision had been taken to found a college; if a house was not soon purchased enthusiasm was likely to fade and the impetus that had carried through the resolution lose its force.

The committee had left it to Elizabeth Brunner to conduct the negotiations with the B.B.C. but the official with whom she was in correspondence seemed unable to appreciate that the W.I. were in a hurry. Finally, feeling that she was getting nowhere, she decided to go over his head and see Sir William Haley, the Director-General.

Unfortunately, the day before her appointment she was stung on the finger by a bee, while working in the garden. Soon afterwards her throat began to swell and she was rushed off to the cottage hospital, given an adrenalin injection and kept there for the night.

The next morning, still swollen, but determined to keep her appointment, she set off for London. Arriving at the B.B.C. she stepped into the lift and found, to her dismay, that she was ascending to Sir William's office in company with the official she had decided to by-pass.

Sir William was friendly and helpful, but even this direct approach did not produce the desired information and the idea of buying Wood Eaton was reluctantly abandoned.

The 1946 Annual General Meeting was a memorable one. The Queen, who was president of Sandringham W.I., came on the first day and paid a special tribute to Lady Denman, congratulating her on all that the W.Is had accomplished under her leadership, both in peace and war. On the second day, after speeches from two women M.Ps, Ellen Wilkinson and Megan Lloyd George, Nancy Tennant broke the news that Lady Denman had decided not to stand again for the Chairmanship.

The announcement drew a gasp of surprise and dismay from the 3,000 women in the hall, for apart from the Executive no one had known of the decision.

"Although she would wish the success of the Movement to be attributed to the work of members as a whole, yet I am certain it would never have acquired the character it has without her . . ." Miss Tennant said, in a moving tribute to the woman who had led the W.Is so wisely and well for nearly thirty years.

Shortly before the meeting ended Lady Albemarle, Lady Denman's heir apparent, went to the microphone. Clever, attractive, in her early forties, she was Lady Denman's own choice as her successor, a choice later endorsed by the Executive.

"Suggestions have been coming in all the afternoon of ways in which we can keep Lady Denman's name in perpetual association with the work of the W.Is" she said. "The most popular is that the Women's Institute College should be known as Denman College. We want this to be a memorial of the sort that would appeal to her."

Amidst shouts of approval and the waving of voting cards Lady Denman stood up and replied, smiling: "Thank you. I think that is a lovely idea!"

It had been a great disappointment to the College Sub-committee that they would not be able to tell the A.G.M. that they had found a house but they did have some good news. As Chairman of the committee it was Elizabeth Brunner's job to launch the £60,000 appeal for the purchase, equipment and endowment of the College. Before doing so she was able to announce that the Carnegie United Kingdom Trust were prepared to make a grant of up to £20,000 to the College Fund, provided the W.Is gave a similar amount.

The College would be a centre for conferences and all branches of W.I. work, practical and cultural, she told the meeting. It would house 30 students, with the possibility of later enlargement to bring the numbers up to 60.

At about this time Purley Park, a house near Reading had come on to the market at a very reasonable price. Lady Denman had been one of the first to see it and felt it would do very well. Other members of the committee were less enthusiastic. It was too far from any village, they said and too close to the railway line. Meanwhile, fearing they might lose what seemed to her a bargain, Lady Denman had put down the deposit out of her own pocket.

Convinced that Purley Park was not the right house for the College, Diana Albemarle felt she must speak against it when the question of whether to make a definite offer came up before the committee; but to do so was a considerable embarrassment to her since it meant that almost her first action in becoming Chairman was to oppose the former Chairman.

Elizabeth Brunner was also against Purley Park and so were two other members of the committee. The matter was put to the vote and the proposal to purchase lost. It was characteristic of Lady Denman that she took this decision in good part.

It was not long after this that a Berkshire member rang up Mrs Methuen to say that her husband, an estate agent, had a property in Berkshire on his books. It was called Marcham Park and he thought it might be what the W.I. wanted. The description sounded promising so Mrs Methuen at once got in touch with Elizabeth Brunner, who lived not far away, and asked her if she would have a look at it.

As it happened both Elizabeth Brunner and Diana Albemarle were attending a W.I. residential school in Oxford that week, on the theme "Leisure and Pleasure", so they decided to drive over to Marcham together, taking with them Sir Ernest Barker, a well-known educationalist who was one of the lecturers.

It was a fine, warm day. The pleasant, gently undulating countryside looked its best, dressed out in the brilliance of high summer; the little grey stone village of Marcham was as peaceful and rural as any W.I. member could wish. Turning off the village street they drove down a lane, through a stone gateway and pulled up before a handsome, late Georgian mansion built of honey-coloured stone. Great trees spread their patterned shadows over what had once been smooth lawns; a stream winding its way through the grounds widened out into an expanse of water away on the far side of the house; beyond were meadows and woodland.

The R.A.F. had used the house as an administrative centre for plans and photographs throughout the war; the tall downstair windows had all been blacked out with paint for security reasons. There were army huts in the grounds and a concrete blockhouse. But these were only temporary defacements and in general the property had suffered little damage.

They were shown round the house by William Blackwell, a local man who had been employed on the estate before the war, and kept on by the R.A.F. who were still in occupation. Built in 1820 on the site of a much earlier house for Thomas Duffield and his wife Emily, who had inherited the estate from her father, it had belonged to the Duffield family until 1938, when it had been bought and modernized by a Mr Berners.

Delighted with the large, well-proportioned downstair rooms

and the elegant wrought iron staircase, which though not part of the original house was contemporary with it, the inspection party noted that there were ten bedrooms on the first floor, six on the second floor and a reasonable number of bathrooms.

There were other advantages too; outbuildings which could be put into use straight away; good garage space and a large kitchen garden. By the time they had finished the tour they were saying happily to each other: "This is it! We've found a house at last."

CHAPTER VI

The Purchase

The Berners family were asking £15,000. This was the sort of price the National Executive felt they could afford to pay. They were all agreed that the house was just the sort of place they wanted, and provided they could obtain vacant possession fairly soon, they were ready to enter into negotiations to purchase.

The agents were notified, but for two months there was no definite news. Then, in November, word came that the R.A.F. would be out by June 1947, and the committee at once recommended that an offer be made; by December a provisional contract had been signed. The agreed price of £16,000 included Marcham House, 100 acres of land, two cottages let to tenants and the kitchen gardens and glass houses, which were let to a local market gardener.

Now that the Federation were committed to pay this large sum it was important that money for the Fund should come in speedily. It had got off to a pretty good start; by the end of 1946 close on £4,000 had been sent in cash and there were promises of donations amounting to nearly £27,000. No one knew better than the committee the problems of raising money in an institute; but though they might grumble, the members could be relied on to pay up in the end – most of them at least, given a little prompting. There were, too, the new institutes to be brought into the net, for this was a time of great expansion in the Movement with W.I.s being formed at the rate of two or three a week. Membership of existing institutes was rising as well, as women returned to their villages from the Forces and others left their war-time jobs. So a second appeal, to serve as a follow-up, was drafted to go out to the institutes as soon as the purchase was completed.

Optimistically, the committee also looked to the property to make a contribution to its upkeep. Dora Tomkinson pointed out that there was plenty of good timber in the woodlands which could be turned into cash and that the kitchen garden could be run as a profit-making concern when the tenancy ran out. There was also the grazing which could be let for £100 a year.

In March the deal was concluded and the price paid – half of it by the Carnegie U.K. Trust. The Federation was now well and truly committed to its most ambitious venture ever. But if there were cold feet no one admitted to them; such was the enthusiasm and confidence of Elizabeth Brunner and her fellow pioneers they carried everyone along with them.

At this stage the *ad hoc* committee was disbanded, since it had done the job it was set up to do; or rather it changed its name and became the Denman College House Committee. Elizabeth Brunner continued as chairman, and apart from Adeline Vernon who had not stood for the Executive that year, the original members remained. The committee was further strengthened by three newcomers, Lady Worsley-Taylor, Mrs Joan Yeo, the new chairman of the N.F.W.I. Education Sub-Committee and the Berkshire Federation's honorary treasurer, Miss Boddy to act as a link between the College and the Berkshire W.I.s. As National Chairman Lady Albemarle was an *ex officio* member.

Young, forward-looking, an Oxford graduate with a degree in history, Joan Yeo had joined the W.I. in the thirties and had quickly become interested in its educational side. Anyone who combines administrative ability with enthusiasm for work is likely to be spotted for promotion in the Movement before long, and Mrs Yeo was no exception. Elected to the National Executive during the war, she was a supporter of the W.I. College project from the start; after Mrs Vernon's retirement her academic interests, organizing ability and talent for getting along with people made her the obvious choice as the new Chairman of Education.

The new committee's terms of reference were to advise the Executive on all matters concerning the College and be responsible "for such matters of detailed administration as the Executive should decide". In other words, its business was to establish the College as a going concern and make sure that it was efficiently run – bearing in mind that the Executive would still have the final say on what was proposed.

As there was obviously going to be a great deal of secretarial work Margaret Bucknall (sister of Barry Bucknall of TV fame) was seconded from Headquarters' staff as full-time secretary.

Eager to start on the furnishing and equipping of the College, the committee found themselves confronted with all manner of problems connected with the estate that needed their urgent attention. The garden was a wilderness, a blockhouse spoilt the view from the dining-room windows and there was barbed wire all over the place. Dora Tomkinson had found an experienced woman gardener who was willing to come for £4 a week, plus accommodation, but, as the tenant in the gardener's cottage was unwilling to move, where was she to live?

Fortunately a furnished cottage was eventually found in the village, so Miss Clarke, the new gardener, was able to start work by April, and two German prisoners of war were taken on to help her. Meanwhile a forestry expert reported that the best of the timber in the surrounding woodlands had been already sold.

The stables, built shortly before the war but never used for horses, had been utilised by the R.A.F. as a gas mask store. The committee's idea was to convert them into extra bedrooms, but here they ran into a new difficulty. The local builder was sorry, but he would not have any labour available before 1948; in any case no building work could be done without a licence.

The need for licences and permits and the difficulty of getting them was to haunt the committee for months to come. They engaged Mr A. L. N. Russell, a London architect, who drew up plans for various structural alterations to the house, estimated at some £12,000 but was doubtful that the Ministry of Works would grant the necessary licence. They also asked the local authority for permission to modernize the gardener's cottage – essential work, in their opinion – but were turned down.

The institutes had all been circulated with the news of the purchase of Marcham Park and at the same time reminded that their help was needed in cash and kind. One result of this was a spate of requests from W.Is asking if they could come and visit Marcham for their summer outing.

It seemed a shame to say "no", but what with the garden non-existent, trees growing out of the fountain and the windows not yet stripped of their gloomy black-out paint, the committee felt it wiser to suggest that they wait a while.

Along with the donations to the College Fund came offers of gifts, not all of which fell into the "just what we wanted" category. A rule had already been made (and is still in force) that all gifts must be considered by the committee. A discreet entry in the minutes in 1945 noted: "Acceptance or refusal would need careful handling". No doubt something of an understatement.

CHAPTER VII

Operation Frolic

In June the R.A.F. moved out, as they had promised and the work of restoring the house to its former elegance could begin. A man about the place was clearly needed and kind, helpful William Blackwell the obvious choice. He was engaged as estate steward, and was to prove an invaluable servant to the College for many years.

That summer Diana Albemarle, Elizabeth Brunner and Frances Farrer, the N.F.W.I. General Secretary, went in a deputation to the Ministry of Education to ask for a grant towards the cost of furnishing and equipping the College. Much to their disappointment they were turned down. The Ministry was interested in their plans and sympathetic to their purpose, but it could not make a direct grant to the College itself. On the other hand it could give grant-aid to the National Federation for its educational work, once the College was established.

Although the interview brought no immediate promise of cash it was helpful in another direction, for the deputation was given permission to quote the Ministry as approving their application for a building licence – at that time very hard to come by indeed. But furniture, still tightly rationed, was another matter. "The situation there is far from rosy," they were told.

At this time the N.F.W.I. had no press and publicity sub-committee; the view that publicity for the W.Is wasn't really necessary and was perhaps rather vulgar still being held in some quarters. However, it was realized that the institutes should be kept in the picture as much as possible as far as the College was concerned, and that hand-outs to the Press had their use for this purpose. *Home and Country* was, naturally, made use of, but unfortunately by no means all members were subscribers.

So to spread the word as widely as possible two young and personable members of the Headquarters staff, Miss Edith Leathart, who had replaced Cecily McCall as Organizer to the Education Sub-committee, and Miss Lucy Lea, had the job of travelling around the country giving talks on the College at county W.I. meetings, group gatherings, and similar events, during the next two years.

This was, in fact, a public relations exercise and it proved a great success. Wherever they went the two girls found tremendous enthusiasm for the College. In the grey aftermath of war it represented a brave new world where women could escape from the dreary old round of household chores. As students (a magical word to many who had been denied secondary education) they would recapture youth and enthusiasm, learn things they had always wanted to learn, use their brains and prove to themselves they *could* learn.

Now and then they did encounter some opposition, but when objections were raised the grounds were usually personal ones, such as the old grumble: "Why should I contribute to something I shall never use?" There were others who, while not objecting to the idea of a College, saw it as something meant for other people, and could not imagine ever overcoming the practical difficulties of getting away from home to attend a course.

Often, when Edith Leathart and Lucy Lea had more bookings than they could cope with, members of the Executive helped out.

In July 1947 Elizabeth Brunner and Joan Yeo went off together on a busman's holiday to Denmark to visit some of the Danish Folk Schools. While they enjoyed the trip and were hospitably received they thought the schools pretty bleak and devoid of creature comforts. On the whole the exercise was not a lot of help with their current problems.

One of the most daunting of these was the preparation of the programme of courses and syllabuses – a job calling for a good deal of professional expertise.

When the committee had first been formed the idea had been put forward that there should be a Board of Governors which would include some professional educationalists. This had been turned down on the grounds that the W.I. should manage its own affairs. Fortunately there were a number of friendly academics who were willing to give help and advice without being offered "a seat on the Board", and in the years to come many continued to do so with great generosity.

Inevitably the early programmes were a compromise between the intellectuals who wanted to offer the more academic courses and those more interested in practical skills; the latter arguing, not without reason, that these were the courses the majority wanted.

With the various sub-committees all eager that the activities they represented should have a fair share of the first year's programme the Executive fell back on the well-tried democratic course of inviting all interested parties to a conference, and to ensure the right spirit they invited Sir Richard Livingstone to be the main speaker. This conference was held in December 1947. Views having thus been aired and points made, the programme was thereafter carefully pieced together and eventually a copy went to every W.I. – at that time close on 7,000.

Application for a building licence had been sent off to the Ministry of Works in September. In October Elizabeth Brunner reported to her committee that she had made "regular visits of enquiry to the Ministry of Works" and that the application had the full support of Major-General Wilson, the area representative of the Ministry of Education in connection with building licences. But all to no avail; in November came the news that the building licence had been refused, on the grounds that there was insufficient labour in the Abingdon area. Anxious to handle the contract the builder promptly declared that he had all the labour he needed for the work, so a fresh application was made, backed once again by General Wilson, but this too was turned down.

Disappointed, but refusing to be discouraged, the committee decided to make the best of the house as it was. By putting up to four beds in the largest rooms and making others into double bedrooms it would be possible to accommodate thirty students. Meanwhile they applied for an urgency licence to carry out repairs to the roof and sewage plant – an application which was granted.

A number of counties had already volunteered to furnish a bedroom, following an appeal in *Home and Country* for help in furnishing the College. Now they had to be told that some must share a room. This decision was not very popular amongst the paired counties; however they put a good face on it and agreed to co-operate. One of the largest rooms was given to the Welsh counties and Monmouthshire; Warwickshire was teamed up with Worcestershire, Dorset with Somerset, Oxfordshire with Middlesex. Yorkshire, the largest county federation, had a big room to itself. Smaller rooms, and those on the top floor, were allocated to individual counties. There would, in any case, be more rooms to furnish when the licence to convert the stables was finally granted.

Furnishing, in this context, meant providing curtains, rugs, bed-spreads, cushions or chair seats, plus any attractive extras that seemed suitable. Lightwood utility furniture was provided by the College, and Elizabeth Brunner had, herself, made sure that the beds were comfortable. Having experienced "academic" beds while attending W.I. residential schools at various educational establishments, she was determined that those provided at Denman should be well-sprung and wide enough to accommodate middle-aged bodies.

As befitted the county which had put forward the W.I. College resolution, Oxfordshire had volunteered to contribute the furnishings of the library in memory of Grace Hadow, who had died in 1940 and who had been a distinguished scholar and an Oxford don as well as the N.F.W.I's first Vice-Chairman. Miss Hadow's portrait, presented by the Oxfordshire Federation, now hangs over the fireplace in this room.

From the East Anglian counties came the offer to furnish the entrance hall; Staffordshire volunteered to supply all the crockery for the dining room; Wiltshire sent several hundred clothing coupons (household linen was still rationed) and West Kent sent along a caravan to be used for any purpose the committee saw fit.

So it went on; gifts and offers of gifts poured in month after month and not only from W.I. members. The International Wool Secretariat gave the curtains and felt carpet for the library; through the good offices of the Methuen family a shipping firm agreed to supply blankets at wholesale price and the Berners family offered the loan of a family portrait. This was an oil painting of Emily Elwes, who ran away to Gretna Green with Thomas Duffield, a local M.P., in defiance of the wishes of her father, an eccentric eighteenth-century squire. Later she became reconciled to her family and inherited her father's fortune and the Marcham estates.

This charming picture hung for many years in the drawing room, but has now been returned to the Duffield family.

With so many gifts of furniture and equipment the committee

found, much to their satisfaction, that their estimate of £4,000 for furnishing the College was too high; on the other hand putting the garden and grounds into order was proving more expensive than they had expected. By the beginning of 1947 some £2,000 had already been spent, but as the tenant had given up the kitchen garden and glasshouses in November, Dora Tomkinson was hoping that these would soon be showing a useful profit.

Happily there was now quite a lot of money in the bank. In less than two years 4,000 institutes had contributed £41,000 to the Denman College Fund, and as there were already well over 6,000 institutes in existence and new ones were being formed at the rate of two or three hundred a year, the committee felt they could reasonably expect that the target of £60,000 would soon be reached.

A sizeable part of the fund would, certainly, be needed to finance new buildings and improvements, when the Ministry of Works and the local authority relented over granting the necessary licences. Already a good deal had had to be spent on essential repairs, redecoration, and so on, but nevertheless it was thought that when all was paid there would still be enough left to produce sufficient income to subsidize the courses.

By the end of April the house had been redecorated and the garden and grounds were considered tidy enough to be shown. Institutes that had written asking if they could bring their members to see the College were told they were welcome to do so that summer; but first there was a full scale private view laid on for 750 delegates to the A.G.M.

To transport this regiment of women from London to Marcham, conduct them round the College and grounds, feed them and return them to base was a formidable task. It says something for the courage of the committee that they were prepared to attempt it, but they felt that the opportunity of showing the College to the delegates, so that they could go back to their villages with a first-hand account, was too good to miss.

On occasions such as these W.I. husbands are apt to find themselves seconded to the organizing committee. By a lucky chance Colonel Yeo, Joan Yeo's husband, was available. As he had been O.C. troop movement on the Clyde during the war, the organization of "Movement Frolic", as he christened the operation, was child's play to him.

In collaboration with Betty Christmas, who had by this time been provisionally chosen as Denman's First Warden, he drew up a time-table, worked out in detail on military lines.

Twenty-four coaches, each carrying thirty-two passengers were scheduled to depart from London in groups of three at half-hourly intervals. Each group, identifiable by different coloured tickets, was allowed two and a half hours to tour the College and grounds and have a meal and an hour's rest before "embussing" for the return journey. In a list of "points for consideration" accompanying his time-table, the Colonel suggested that a "Queen Trouble-Shooter" or M.C. with junior assistant, should be at Marcham throughout the operation in a supervisory role with no other special function; that if it was too wet for sitting in the garden a large rest room should be provided labelled "Me Pore Feet", and that two toilet rolls should be placed in each toilet, plus some in reserve.

Thanks to Colonel Yeo, Betty Christmas and a regiment of W.I. helpers, "Movement Frolic" went off according to plan. It was the first of many mammoth parties to be held at Denman.

CHAPTER VIII

A Warden is Appointed

Once the date for the official opening had been fixed for September 24th of that year it was clearly time to start looking around for a Warden. The sort of woman the Executive had in mind was someone who would be able to control and organize the running of the College and at the same time make the shyest W.I. member feel at home. They wanted someone efficient, but knew that a friendly and sympathetic personality was equally important and although they were not insisting on a university degree they did rather expect that the warden of their choice would have a good academic background.

The post had still to be advertised when someone said: "What about Miss Christmas?"

Elizabeth Christmas (or Betty as she was known to her friends) was then thirty-seven and had been N.F.W.I. General Organizer for eight years. It was true that she had no academic qualifications for the job, but her intelligence and organizing ability had been proved over the years, and she was immensely popular amongst the institutes. She had also carried out a highly successful coast to coast tour of the Canadian W.Is in 1945 on behalf of the Ministry of Information.

There is a story that when this tour was being fixed up the person responsible for making the arrangements at the Canadian end was called to the Foreign Office in Ottawa one morning and ticked off for having a cable sent to her in code.

"You ought to know", they told her crossly, "that no one is allowed to receive unauthorised cables in code. Now will you please tell us what this cable addressed to you means, because our experts have been unable to decipher it?"

The cable read "Christmas comes in July".

"I'm the little girl from the country who made good," Betty Christmas once said to another member of the N.F.W.I. staff.

The daughter of a village postmaster, she joined Bures W.I. in West Suffolk when she was sixteen. She was pretty, lively and intelligent, already showing a gift for organization and it was not long before she became assistant secretary. Impressed by her abilities the President, Mrs Margaret Hitchcock, who was also a member of the National Executive, felt sure she would go far. Acting was one of her great interests and soon she was playing leading parts in local drama productions.

After a few years working as a secretary in the neighbourhood of Bures she began to look further afield. On the recommendation of Mrs Hitchcock she was offered a job at N.F.W.I. Headquarters in the accounts department and came to live in London and work at Eccleston Street. After a couple of years she decided to go to South Africa, but in 1935 she returned to England to take up an appointment as County Secretary of the Buckinghamshire W.I. Federation; there she stayed until 1940, when she applied for the post of General Organizer to the N.F.W.I. and got the job.

As she travelled around the country during the years that followed, giving help and advice to county federations and meeting the members at all levels, Betty Christmas made innumerable friends. Her warmth of manner sprang from a deep love of people, and her zest for life made it fun to be in her company. She was essentially a practical person, loving to plan and organize; never short of ideas. But perhaps her greatest asset as Warden of Denman College was a talent amounting almost to genius, for infecting others with her own enthusiasm for the job in hand.

Despite these qualities she was modest about her abilities. When she learned that she would be considered for the post of warden she confessed to a friend that she was not at all sure that she was the right person.

After all, she pointed out, she had never kept house for anyone and the prospect of running a household of fifty was daunting.

When her appointment as prospective Warden of Denman was confirmed in April 1948 she at once began to look around for her staff. It was during the A.G.M. that year that she made her first choice.

Miss Christina Beckton, secretary of the Cumberland Federation for twelve years, had come up to London to the A.G.M. with her county delegation. A capable, good-humoured young woman, who enjoyed her work, she certainly had no thought in her head of applying for a job at Denman College at this time, but when Betty Christmas, whom she already knew well, took her aside and asked her for her help in running Denman College, she felt she could not refuse, even though it meant leaving her mother, with whom she was living, her home and all her friends. "I wouldn't have done it for anyone but Betty!" she said later.

So she applied for the post of College Secretary and was appointed to start work on September 1st. Soon after this Miss Messer, who was leaving her job of Matron at Radbrook College at the end of the summer, when the two principals, Miss Bode and Miss Hutton, retired, agreed to become resident housekeeper.

The next to be appointed was Miss Barbara Lilley, who had recently resigned from her job as County Secretary of the Hereford-shire Federation, in order to be near her father, Canon Lilley, who lived in Oxford. As she had taken a cottage only a few miles away from Marcham she was asked if she would be willing to help with the secretarial work at the College. As a result she became Warden's Secretary and remained a dedicated member of the staff for the next twelve years.

At this stage it was not thought necessary to appoint a resident tutor, nor was there officially a Bursar. The administrative staff, therefore, consisted of Betty Christmas, Christina Beckton and Barbara Lilley, plus a local girl to help with the typing. On the domestic side the resident staff were Miss Messer, Mrs Parker, the cook and two Swedish girls who had come over to learn English and been put in touch with Denman College through the N.F.W.I's international links.

When these two Swedish girls came to see the College they couldn't make up their minds whether to stay and work there or not. Still undecided they went for a walk round the estate and on their return announced that they had put the decision to the toss of a coin and were going to stay!

Up till June 1948 Elizabeth Brunner's committee had held their meetings at the N.F.W.I. Headquarters in London. There was still a prodigious amount to be done before opening day and the com-mittee would often sit for hours. So much that was needed was in short supply (it took nearly a year to get a new lawn mower) and there were endless delays and difficulties in obtaining permits to carry out repairs and improvements.

As well as seeing that all was ready for the official opening in September, they had to deal with such problems as how to obtain possession of the estate's best cottage when the sitting tenant was determined to remain there, and what to do with the gun emplacements and hideous blockhouse, which the War Office refused to move.

The house was still empty of furniture when the committee decided that they had better hold their meetings there, instead of in London, so William Blackwell cut up logs to serve as chairs. Improvization was the order of the day. Curtains for the dining room were made up from table cloths that had been used by Lady Denman in Government House when her husband was Governor-General of Australia. In some of the other rooms black-out curtains, bleached to a tolerable shade of gold, did service for several years.

As the summer wore on the sleepy little village of Marcham grew accustomed to seeing coach loads of women passing through the village on their way to and from Marcham Park. Between April and mid-September nearly 7,000 W.I. members visited the College. Volunteer guides from Berkshire and Oxfordshire W.Is showed them round and Blackwell and Kinchin the gardener and woodman, found themselves answering innumerable questions on local flora and fauna. Coloured postcards of the College were on sale to help the funds and a model, made by Abingdon County Secondary School was on display.

One fascinating job that fell to the lot of Mrs Yeo and Lady Listowel (another good friend of the College) that summer was selecting pictures from the Victoria and Albert Museum for the main rooms and the first floor landing, the committee having discovered that as an "accredited training college" Denman was entitled to have pictures on loan from the museum for up to six months at a time, a concession that has continued to the present day. And in the dining-room, thanks to the good offices of Mrs Edward Bawden, another member of the committee, there were pictures and drawings lent by contemporary artists, such as Edward Bawden and John Aldridge.

As a Governor of the Victoria and Albert, Lady Listowel was also able to arrange for some superb examples of needlework, from the V. and A. Loan Collection of Embroideries, to be shown at Denman and on another occasion a rich and splendid display of rugs. This readiness on the part of curators and other distinguished experts to help the College was tremendously encouraging to Elizabeth Brunner and her committee, making them feel that Denman was now accepted as an institution really worthy of support.

In the last weeks before opening day the College buzzed with activity. The resident staff moved in and immediately found themselves working from dawn till dusk. Marcham W.I. had been re-formed and a sewing party of local members came regularly to help make curtains and deal with anything else that needed stitching; committee members rushed back and forth, those with families at home for the summer holidays, torn between domestic demands and their by now total involvement in the successful launching of their College. Finally a working party of sixteen volunteers, recruited by Betty Christmas from W.Is all over the country moved in and spent the last seven days scrubbing, touching up paintwork, hanging pictures, weeding the garden and generally tackling any job that needed doing.

On the Thursday, the eve of the official opening, Elizabeth Brunner walked through the rooms to see that all was as it should be; perhaps too, to savour the satisfaction of achievement.

Green-gold mats made from Norfolk reeds by Norfolk members covered the floor of the entrance hall; tall vases of flowers lent colour and freshness. There was a big, comfortable chesterfield by the open fireplace; the grandfather clock ticked a welcome.

The drawing room, with its finely proportioned windows, its beautiful chrystal chandelier, its elegant French eighteenth-century furniture (a gift from Lady Denman), its grand piano and comfortable sofas, offered rest and relaxation. It was a room that would have graced any stately home. Here had been hung the portrait of the romantic Emily Elwes.

In the library there were comfortable chairs and shelves already well-stocked, each book bearing the bookplate designed for the College by Reynolds Stone. Next came the lecture room where an exhibition of craft work had been set out. Everything there was a gift to the College – bedspreads, mats, curtains and so on – to be used when the extensions were built.

The effect in the dining-room was bright and modern; the separate Pel tables were red-topped with grey frames, the Pel chairs the same grey. This was where Lady Denman's Government House table cloths had been hung as curtains, made gay by prancing red and blue unicorns handblocked on the material by Nancy Nicholson.

Beyond was the kitchen, full of gleaming new equipment, much of it given, including the refrigerator. In the store cupboards stood rows of preserves contributed by members.

Upstairs the bedrooms with their carefully planned colour schemes, hand-made quilts and beautifully embroidered bedspreads, awaited their first occupants. There were to be thirty-two members staying in the College that week-end, with others accommodated nearby.

The title of the inaugural course summed up the aims and purpose of Denman: "The Education of the Countrywoman through the W.Is".

If any of the county federations still did not understand what Denman was all about this was their chance to find out, for each had been invited to send one member to attend the opening and the introductory course, and those whose counties had furnished a bedroom, or part of one would have the privilege of being the first member to sleep there.

CHAPTER IX

Sir Richard Cuts the Ribbon

The next morning was cloudless. The dew on the newly mown lawns sparkled in the sunshine, the great trees stood sharply outlined in the clear bright light, their branches unstirring. It was a perfect autumn day.

The Press were the first to arrive. They were brought by coach from Abingdon station and taken on a conducted tour of the house; they asked numerous questions and were especially fascinated by the examples of traditional craftwork in the bedrooms and by the small, personal touches that gave the rooms so much charm and individuality. Even the linen cupboard was opened for their benefit and the women reporters' eyes widened with envy at the sight of the piles of crisp new sheets sent by Canadian W.Is, and the big fluffy blankets bought with clothing coupons given by members.

A tour of the garden followed, then a buffet luncheon. Meanwhile coach-loads of W.I. members were on their way to Marcham from London for the reception in the early afternoon. A number of V.I.Ps, including academics who had already given the College their blessing and support (or, it was hoped, would do so in the future) had also been invited.

Rather than risk having the opening ruined by a downpour it had been decided to have the speeches in the big garage by the main gate. It was hardly a perfect setting for a formal occasion, but it had been whitewashed and made gay with vases of autumn flowers, and Blackwell had knocked up a platform from Ministry of Works packing cases.

Shortly before the ceremony was due to begin he spotted a shabby looking car parked right in front of the garage, despite the "No Parking" notices; so he went over to remonstrate.

"Well, of course, if you don't *want* the B.B.C. here we'll go," the young man in charge said, with a grin.

By two-thirty the guests had all been received by Lady Albemarle, as Chairman of the National Federation, and by Miss

Christmas as Warden, and it was time for the speeches. Sir Richard Livingstone had been invited to perform the opening ceremony; in introducing him Diana Albemarle summed up in a sentence the feelings of her fellow members.

"This", she said, "is the moment of fruition!"

The discourses of V.I.Ps on such occasions seldom bear repeating but Sir Richard's speech must be quoted here, at least in part, for it expressed so perfectly the beliefs and hopes of those who had pioneered Denman.

He began by likening life to a corridor with rooms opening off, filled with the treasures of history, art, music, literature and science. "But how many people," he asked, "walk down the corridor, entering but few of the rooms?"

It was, he said, the business of education to help people to do the things they wanted to do, but could not without help . . . "read books, enjoy music and art, grow flowers and vegetables, decorate a house, do needlework, bring up children, understand engines or the stars, and much else."

"Many people do not, or cannot learn at school," he continued. "Anyhow, we discover new interests and needs in later life and want help to pursue them. That is where Denman College comes in. It gives women the chance of learning and thinking about things which, when young, they could not study and did not think about studying. But one can't do that sort of thing at home. One needs a place like this to get away from household duties and worries and give one's whole time to the business in hand."

He said much more, picturing individuals returning home to pass on their knowledge, so that enlightenment spread in the villages, then he ended with congratulations to the women who had had "the imagination, the faith and enterprise and energy, the patience and perseverance" to carry through the idea.

When he sat down Lady Denman rose to thank him and, at the same time, to reaffirm her faith in countrywomen in general; after which it was Elizabeth Brunner's turn to propose a general vote of thanks to everyone who had helped. The platform party then led the way to the house where a ribbon had been stretched across the front door, secured on either side by a spray of flowers.

Sir Richard was handed a pair of scissors and everyone waited for the ceremonial cutting of the ribbon. There was a moment's pause while he considered the task before him; then bending forward he carefully snipped through the ribbon as close as possible to the flowers. As he said later, his Scottish blood would not let him waste more of such a fine piece of ribbon than he could help.

Everything had gone splendidly; it only remained for tea to be served to the two hundred and fifty guests. This job had been handed over to a local caterer, so as to give the committee and hard-pressed staff a break. Unfortunately, although he had assured the committee he would be able to cope, the caterer's organization broke down under the strain, so Elizabeth Brunner, Dora Tomkinson and Joan Yeo rolled up their sleeves and went to work in the tea tent.

After dinner that evening, the forty-three members who were staying for the course gathered in the big lecture room to hear Dr Adams, head of the National Council for Social Service, and an old friend of the late Grace Hadow, give the inaugural lecture which, sensing the exhaustion of his audience after a long and strenuous day, he insisted was not a lecture at all. Mostly he talked of poetry, in particular of the American poet, Stephen Vincent Benet's poem "John Brown's Body", and he declared himself touched by the beginnings of the Denman College library. Later there was music, with Miss Margaret Deneke (sister of Miss Helena Deneke) at the piano.

The next morning after breakfast, the students settled down to their first study session. They heard about the educational work of the W.Is from Esther Neville Smith, and from a county director of education learnt of the opportunities provided by L.E.A. Their afternoon was left free but they assembled again after tea to hear the Principal of St Anne's Society in Oxford on the purpose of education.

After so much intellectual effort they were treated to a party in the evening. The next morning was left free for those who might wish to go to church.

But on Sunday afternoon it was back to work again for the last session, a talk on Denman College by the Warden, followed by a discussion on how to make the best use of the College, and a summing up of the whole course by Mrs Vernon.

"It was a week-end of delight," wrote one enthusiastic student in a letter to *Home and Country*. "Those of us who were privileged to attend this first course will be envied by all other members . . ."

By Monday morning the College was empty except for the staff – but not for long; that same evening thirty-two students were due to arrive for a five-day "Country Housewives" course, a potpourri of domestic skills and cultural interests designed for general appeal.

This was an "A" course, intended for ordinary members who paid for themselves (or were paid for by their own W.I. from a Bursary Fund) as opposed to the "B" courses for members sponsored by their county federations on the understanding that they would be prepared to pass on what they had learned to other members on their return. The fees for both "A" and "B" courses were fifteen shillings a night, including full board, plus a tuition fee of five shillings. This was well below the economic cost, but it had always been the intention to subsidize the courses so that they would be within nearly everyone's means.

To be on the safe side and make sure of filling the College, the programme for the first three months was largely composed of "B" courses; there was one for handicraft teachers, one for choir leaders and conductors, one for W.I. Market organizers, and so on; while the ordinary member had the choice of four "Country Housewives'" courses, one "Christmas Course" and one (and how dated it now sounds) on "The Colonial Empire".

No one knew what sort of members would be coming on that first "A" course, but at least there had been plenty of applications – more than could be accepted. In any case, busy as they were with the clearing up after the departure of the week-end guests the staff had little time for speculation. Mondays, as they were soon to learn, were always one long rush.

All the same, as the time drew near for the students' arrival they began to suffer the same last minute doubts and fears of the young hostess awaiting her guests for her first big party. Suppose hardly anyone turned up?

Then the first taxi from the station pulled up at the front door and the Warden, waiting in the hall to give her welcome, turned to Christina Beckton and murmured, almost with awe: "They're really here!"

CHAPTER X

Running In

There were sessions on cookery and flower arrangement and talks on music and history for the students who came to that first Country Housewives' course. From Margaret Bucknall, who had worked at the Design Centre before joining the N.F.W.I. staff, they learnt about design in the home and there was an outing to Oxford. In the friendly, easy atmosphere that Betty Christmas could always create, the shy soon thawed.

For many of the students the business of getting away from home had taken a good deal of organizing. Some were suffering from feelings of guilt at having left their families to fend for themselves (a not unusual state of mind in Denman students); others were wondering uneasily if the neighbour or relative they'd left in charge would be able to manage, but within a few hours these worries were forgotten.

The pattern of study sessions from 9.30 to 12.45 in the mornings, with a mid-morning coffee break in the hall; a free afternoon, followed by a ninety-minute session between tea and supper and a final hour's session after supper was established at this time and has remained more or less the same ever since. So also has the custom of a concert on the Thursday evening for all the students staying at the College, or some sort of musical or dramatic entertainment.

Very often Miss Margaret Deneke, an accomplished pianist, would be at the piano on Thursday evenings. Like her sister, Helena Deneke, she had supported the idea of the College from the beginning. She loved coming to Denman to play and knew very well that once she sat down at the piano she would forget all about the time, so she would tell the taxi driver who always brought her to and from Oxford: "Now Arthur, you're to come in and fetch me from the piano when it's time for me to go!" And around ten o'clock, Arthur, embarrassed but conscientious, would appear in the drawing room.

The length of the courses was to some extent dictated by rationing regulations; these required residential establishments to collect rations from guests who stayed more than five days. Apart from this, it was thought that from tea-time on the Monday to after breakfast on the Friday morning would best suit most members, especially those with families who would probably find it difficult to be away from home over the week-end. This did not mean that the College would not sometimes run longer or shorter courses, but then, as now, the majority were planned to last four days.

A practice established from the start was to invite one member to act as Chairman throughout the course. Later, when two or more courses were run concurrently there would be an overall "College Chairman" as well as a chairman for each course.

Her duties, laid down at that time, were three-fold; she was expected to act as hostess, introduce the speakers and encourage discussion on the talks or demonstrations; to provide "a thread of continuity between talks, excursions and demonstrations" and "relate the content of the course to the every-day experience of members" where possible linking it with their knowledge of the W.I. Movement and opportunities for continuing their studies in their own counties.

Obviously an experienced member of some authority was needed for this role. Other essential qualities were friendliness, patience and tact – not to mention a strong right arm for pouring out large numbers of cups of tea! Usually chairmen were (and still are) present or past members of the N.F.W.I. Executive Committee or one of the National Sub-committees, or a County Committee. Mrs Vernon, Mrs Neville-Smith, Miss Corbett and Mrs Yeo, all regularly acted as chairmen for courses on history and the arts in the early days, and sometimes took sessions themselves, as they were well qualified to do.

As a sort of buffer state between staff and students, Denman's College and course chairmen have played an invaluable role. Through attending the study sessions they can gauge both the value of the course to the students and the ability of the lecturers to put their subject over. By being resident in the College they can see whether or not things are going smoothly. For those who serve on the Denman College Committee this first-hand knowledge of how the College functions has been very useful indeed. In the early days it was especially so.

After that first Country Housewives' course ended and the students, declaring that they would all be back again soon had departed, Betty Christmas gave a party for everyone who had helped to make Denman ready for the opening – the indoor and outdoor staff, the W.I. members who had come to scrub and sew, and dig the garden, and the Berkshire and Oxfordshire members who had acted as guides to all the W.I. outings to the College that summer. It was the first of many such parties to be held at Denman during Betty Christmas's wardenship, bringing the staff and members together in a friendly and relaxed atmosphere.

Soon after the official opening the committee heard that the long awaited licence to convert the stables into bedrooms had been granted. This would mean accommodation for another eighteen students and a useful additional income in fees. Good news though it was, much more would need to be done if all the plans for improvements were to be carried out.

Elizabeth Brunner felt that there ought to be a block of single bedrooms for the benefit of those who disliked sharing a room; a staff room was lacking and an office. More accommodation for students meant that a larger dining-room would be needed, and extra cloakrooms.

Another pressing need was for a demonstration kitchen and additional lecture rooms ready for the time when there would be three courses running simultaneously. The possibility of making use of the R.A.F. huts, which were still standing in the grounds, had often been considered, but even if a licence was granted to convert them the scheme looked like proving pretty costly. However, here the College had a piece of good fortune. The Berkshire County Council were looking for somewhere to site a new rural domestic economy school and their R.D.E. Instructress, Miss Doris Cumming, already a good friend of the W.I., suggested that they might get together with the College to work out a scheme for combining to make use of the huts as demonstration kitchens and handicraft rooms.

This idea was warmly welcomed by the committee and negotiations with the Berkshire County Council were begun early in 1949. As might be expected there was a tangle of red tape to be sorted out before any decision could be taken, but with Miss Cumming on their side the Denman Committee hoped that the scheme would go through in the end.

Meanwhile, there were inevitable teething troubles in running the College. The solid fuel boiler kept going out at night, with consequent lack of hot water in the mornings and grumbles from students hoping for hot baths. Too few lavatories meant tedious morning queues. Then there was the problem of feeding the hens Dora Tomkinson had bought to help out the egg ration. The War Agricultural Committee, she complained, would only allow feeding coupons based on the number of resident staff, instead of on the number of students per week, and the hens would never lay on so inadequate a diet.

The hens were finally written off, but before this the Committee decided that the charm of the lake would be enhanced by swans and wrote asking H.M. Swan Keeper if two pairs could be supplied. This request was granted, with the proviso that the College should pay for catching them and their transport, and the swans duly arrived. Unfortunately their tempers did not match their appearance and the only person they would allow near them was Blackwell. In the end, after one pair had pursued Miss Messer, the housekeeper, so ferociously that she had to climb over a wall to escape, they were sent back in disgrace with a request for more docile birds.

A more intractable problem was how to persuade the War Office to remove or pay for the removal of the blockhouse which was spoiling the view from the dining-room window. In the end, after more than two years of correspondence on the subject, plus the intervention of the Local Authority on the N.F.W.I's behalf, the War Office grudgingly offered £15 towards the removal of this eyesore.

By the end of 1948 some four hundred students had attended courses at the College, and applications for the first part of the 1949 programme, which had gone out to the institutes during the autumn, were coming in well. This, and subsequent programmes for some years to come, were drawn up by the N.F.W.I. Education Sub-committee in consultation with the Warden and with the other national sub-committees so that a balance should be kept between all the various interests. But when it came to the actual syllabuses, these were usually the result of Betty Christmas and Joan Yeo putting their heads together.

Amongst the practical courses for the ordinary members ("A" courses) held in 1949 were: Catering, Home Management, Gardening, Fruit Preservation, Soft Toy Making and Smocking. There were also four Country Housewife courses, two for nature lovers, under the heading "Pleasures of the Countryside" and two Christmas courses – corresponding to the Country Housewife course, but with a Christmassy slant.

Academic courses included such titles as "Books and Music", "The Victorian Age", and "Feeding the Hungry World". Predictably, practical courses were the most popular and were taken by the N.F.W.I's own experts; they were also the most expensive to run, for it was usually necessary to limit the numbers to a dozen or so in order to give some individual instruction, whereas up to thirty students could be taken for an academic course. On the other hand the latter were obviously something of a gamble since there was no way of knowing the likely response to a particular subject. As Joan Yeo put it, "we were trying to see how much academic education the W.I. would take".

"Books and Music", in March 1949, was one of the first academic courses to be held. Joan Yeo, who acted as Chairman, jotted down her impressions of some of the twenty-eight students who attended.

There was a twenty-year-old librarian, "very lively with a penetrating intelligence". Several were from Wales; one was "smiling, plump and appreciative", another "seemed scared at the idea of going deeper into our subjects". One student wrote light novels but "was *not* musical". Mrs H. wore a red jacket all the time and "took in all she could get"; Lady K. was "charming and gay".

Some rather baffled the observant Mrs Yeo, including the stoutish, red-faced lady who took no part in any of the discussions, but "rather too much in the singing", and the student from the North who "persisted in liking it *all*", yet gave no clue as to how much she had taken in.

The four-day programme was certainly a pretty concentrated dose of culture. There were several lectures; Miss Rebecca West gave one, Miss Lorna Moore,* a former editor of *Home and Country*, gave another. An Oxford bookseller talked about his job, and an Oxford

---

*Now head of the B.B.C. Talks Department and one of Denman's Educational advisers.

woman don about literature in general. There were also poetry reading, musical appreciation, and recorder playing sessions, a visit to the Bodleian Library and a concert.

After the course was over Joan Yeo noted: "Could the agenda be sent to speakers *before* they come? None of them seem to know into what they were fitting – but they fitted just the same!"

In June, on the day following the A.G.M. in London, the converted stable building, to be known as "The Croft", was officially opened and once again a convoy of coaches was laid on to bring delegates to Marcham for the occasion.

The seven double and two single bedrooms had been furnished by county federations, just as the bedrooms had been in the house itself, and bore the names of the counties on their doors. Most of them were rather small, especially the single rooms, but the skilful use of colour made them seem larger than they were, and in each were many examples of beautiful craft work.

Later the librarian of the Bodleian who had been shown round took the College to task over the fact that a shade on one of the bedside lamps had been made from an old manorial roll! A fact of which everyone had been in ignorance until he pointed it out.

Diana Albemarle was away in Copenhagen, attending a UNESCO conference that month so it fell to Mrs Neville Smith, a Vice-Chairman of the National Federation, to introduce Mr Salter Davies, the Chairman of the Carnegie United Kingdom Trust, who performed the opening ceremony.

In doing so he made it plain that he thought the Trust's contribution to Denman College had been well spent.

"I have never seen," he said, "a more living and striking example of community life in practice than in this beautiful college".

Denman was closed for two weeks in July while the staff dispersed for a well-earned holiday. But if the bedrooms were empty the grounds and main rooms were not. To avoid disturbing the courses it had been decided that the W.I. outings to Denman should take place only during the holiday period, a decision that caused some resentment amongst institutes that had not yet made the trip since it meant that some would have to wait for two or three years. In that July alone 8,000 members visited the College. Day after day coaches blocked the narrow roads and caused traffic hold-ups. One party from Durham even hired a special train. However, the village, now used to W.I. invasions, took it in good part. Some local people had been rather dubious at first about Marcham House being turned into a female college, but when local labour began to be employed and when the resident staff became known and liked in the village doubts soon vanished.

As the W.I. members wandered about the grounds Blackwell and Kinchin were always ready and willing to answer questions about the trees and wild life. Kinchin could show them where the badgers' walk was and Blackwell, who had known the estate all his life could point out the cedar Alexander on the lawn that marks the grave of a Duffield dog and describe how the garden looked in former times. There was a noticeable difference, he thought, between the members who came on the outings at that time and those who came as students. The students were better dressed then; nowadays it seems to him, they all dress equally well.

W.I. memorials were beginning to appear in the garden and grounds; an avenue of limes was planted as a memorial to Mrs Alfred Watt, founder of the W.I. Movement in England and Wales; a herb garden commemorates another well-known member and garden seats have been given by county federations in memory of those to whom they are especially grateful.

One student presented the College with an electric floor polisher in memory of her mother, also a W.I. member. This practical memorial soon became one of the most cherished possessions of Phyllis Gosling, the head housemaid, and has been in use ever since.

Now that the College could take up to fifty students and thus run two or three courses at a time, Betty Christmas felt she must have more staff (while courses were in progress she and Christina Beckton had been working a fourteen-hour day) so Edith Leathart was appointed resident tutor.

The opening of The Croft also meant that the demonstration kitchen had to be sacrificed to provide more dining-room accommodation. By this time it seemed likely that agreement would be reached with the Berkshire County Council to use the huts as an R.D.E. centre, but until then there was nothing for it but to improvise, and so the caravan given by West Kent was turned into a temporary demonstration unit.

CHAPTER XI

One Year Old

"Sam was a great ice-breaker," recalls Margery Roney-Dougal, who was a student on one of the courses at the start of Denman's second year, and who later became a member of the Denman College Committee.

Sam was the friendly black Labrador belonging to Betty Christmas. He had been given to her by Elizabeth Brunner and had quickly become a general favourite.

Mrs Roney-Dougal was then in her thirties, the mother of two children. She had not been nervous at the idea of going to Denman, nevertheless when she arrived at the front door she was suddenly overwhelmed by the horrid sinking feeling she always felt when she went back to the boarding school she had heartily disliked. However, it was too late to turn tail; the door opened and in the cheerful, friendly atmosphere her fears disappeared unnoticed.

She was taking the gardening course and remembers that it combined with a country housewives' course on the first evening for a talk on good design, followed by a general discussion which produced a lively exchange of ideas. The following day she and her fellow gardening students got down to work in the garden budding roses under the supervision of Mary Clarke, the head gardener.

The entertainment on the Thursday evening was home-made, the students getting together to do their share and the staff contributing a flesh-creeping performance of "The Ghost of Denman College".

The noise in the dining-room was "frightful", with some fifty voices competing against the clatter of dishes in a confined space, without sound-proofing. The washing-up rota, which was pinned up in the hall, was accepted cheerfully. Students were also asked to make their beds and mop out their rooms, and to make the beds up with clean sheets before departure – chores which everyone considered reasonable.

Because most of the students on these two courses were of her own age, she remembers particularly an old lady, said to be over seventy, who had never been away from home before, but who came on several more courses.

In Denman's early years it was not unusual for students to remark that this was the first holiday they had had since they were married. Their institutes had given them a Bursary, or they had won one in a draw or competition and had been persuaded, or had determined not to let the opportunity go by. And if they did feel a bit apprehensive about going right away to stay in a college, it was after all part of the W.I. and they'd be amongst their fellow members. Besides, what an adventure for the wife of a farm worker or a miner who had never had the chance to travel further than her nearest market town before. What a story to tell on her return home!

"Oh how wonderful to lift the lid off a dish and not know what's inside!" exclaimed one bursary student on her first evening.

Occasionally there were dramas. On one course a middle-aged student arrived feeling worried and guilty because she had come away when her mother was in a poor state of health. On the second day a telegram arrived for her. Opening it with trembling fingers she promptly collapsed, crying out that poor Mum was dead and it was a judgement on her for coming away.

The telegram read: "Dear Mum passed higher". A sympathetic member of the staff suggested that it might perhaps have a less tragic meaning, and sure enough it was from the student's son who had wired to say he had been successful in his higher school certificate.

Inevitably there were times when arrangements went awry. Edith Leathart had a particularly mortifying experience when, as Tutor, she took a party of students to see the ballet at the Oxford Playhouse. She had just got them all settled in their seats and supplied with programmes when an announcement from the management came over the loud speaker. "Will the W.I. party from Denman College kindly give up their seats as they have come on the wrong day!"

The fact that the muddle was the fault of the box office could not compensate for her agony of embarrassment as she collected her disgruntled party and led them, with many apologies, out of the theatre.

As a matter of policy one or two cultural sessions were included in all courses, in the belief that even if students had come primarily to learn cake icing or rush basketry they would be bound to benefit from two or three hours exposure to culture of one sort or another and might, it was hoped, be thus encouraged to come back for one of the academic courses.

Sad to say it did not always work out that way. Craft students, struggling to finish the work set by their instructors, were apt to prove elusive, if not down-right rebellious, when required to join another course for a musical session, or a reading from Jane Austen. As Tutor it usually fell to Miss Leathart to round up the absentees, and there were times when persuasion failed.

Betty Christmas was not at all well that autumn, although she carried on with her work as usual. Because she loved meeting and talking to the students, and because they were always seeking her out, she was seldom off duty except at the week-ends, and she was also greatly in demand as a speaker on the College at county meetings.

Since her appointment she had identified herself completely with Denman, working untiringly for its success. To her it was far more than a short-stay college where women came to pick up a little knowledge, or learn some skill or craft. She wanted it to be an oasis where people were happy and had fun, staff and students together, without any social barriers – a genuine working community. And to a great extent she succeeded, but so much hard work and dedication took its toll.

At this time she was still living in the house, but was looking forward to having her own cottage in the grounds when the licence was granted to modernize what had once been the butler's cottage.

That December while the College was closed for the vacation, her mother, who was staying with her, died suddenly in the night. Betty Christmas sustained this shock bravely, but her health, already impaired by an as yet undiagnosed disease, suffered as a result. Some months later she was operated on for the removal of a growth.

The staff carried on loyally in her absence and she was soon back at work again, having apparently made a good recovery.

Meanwhile the new programme had gone out and applications for courses were coming in well, particularly for the craft subjects and for "Country Housewives". There was an encouraging response, too, for some of the history and literature courses which were being tried out. A young don from Oxford was the lecturer on many of these and already had an enthusiastic following amongst Denman students.

"He's deep, that Dr Butler," one student was overheard to say to another, "but you *can* understand him."

Despite the opposition of the Chairman of the Berkshire County Council an agreement was finally reached by which the College would lease to the County Council two and a half acres of land and two of the R.A.F. huts and contribute half the capital for turning one of them into a demonstration centre.

That June the N.F.W.I. had the satisfaction of lending Denman to the Carnegie United Kingdom Trust for a week-end conference. It was hoped that other week-end bookings from voluntary organizations would follow and bring in extra money, but for some years these failed to materialise.

Later that summer the N.F.W.I. Executive themselves took over Denman for a week-end, when they gave a house-party for Commonwealth delegates on their way to Copenhagen to attend the Associated Country Women of the World Triennial Conference. This was the first of several such gatherings to be held in the College.

Proud though the Executive were to be able to show off their fine new college to members of countrywomen's organizations from overseas, those concerned with the running of it were very conscious that much still needed to be done. Unfortunately funds were getting low and the decision had to be taken that for the time being the spending had to stop.

Already capital expenditure, plus future commitments amounted to £41,000 and at the end of the year a subsidy of some £2,000 from the National Federation's General Fund was needed in order to balance the accounts. Some of the Executive were not too happy about this, fearing that the cost of running the College might be getting out of hand. It had been hoped that the income from the Endowment Fund would largely bridge the gap between expenditure and income, but this was obviously not going to happen until the Fund, then standing at £27,000, had been built up to £40,000 or more.

Nearly 6,000 institutes had, by this time, sent in donations to the Denman College Fund, which was standing at around £48,000 – £12,000 below the target set in 1946; but there were still 2,000 that had not yet responded, despite appeals in *Home and Country* and all the talks on the College given up and down the country by Betty Christmas and members of the committee.

Since exhortation did not seem to move them it was decided to try a carrot, in the form of an incentive scheme which promised a bursary to all county federations that had subscribed £10 per institute before the end of 1953. This scheme was launched in the autumn of 1951.

Miss Leathart resigned from the College staff in 1950 and early in 1951 Miss Monica Sims (later to become editor of "Woman's Hour") was appointed Tutor. In her early twenties and not long graduated from Oxford, she threw herself into the job with great enthusiasm, enjoying it enormously. Working with Betty Christmas was always fun; it was exciting to meet the distinguished men and women who came to give lectures and she was fascinated by the variety of students.

Her duties ranged from arranging the flowers to helping to plan the courses, taking sessions in literature and sometimes giving a poetry reading. Many years later she was to return to Denman to take a session on "Behind the Scenes at the B.B.C."

Betty Christmas encouraged her staff to mingle with the students as much as they could and loved to do so herself. If an impromptu entertainment was to be put on during the last evening she was always game to take part. On one occasion, during a W.I. Press Correspondents' Course, Mrs Olive Farquharson, who was chairing the course, devised an entertainment for the last evening, in which the various features of a typical women's magazine were personalised, and she remembers how, dressed up in button boots and a feather boa, Betty Christmas stole the show as Aunt Agatha of the Lonely Hearts column.

Years later a member of the staff at that time recalled "Wherever Miss Christmas was there was laughter".

In May 1951 Lady Brunner was elected Chairman of the N.F.W.I. following Lady Albemarle's retirement. It was a popular appointment, but it did mean she was unable to continue as Chairman of the Denman House committee, though she continued to keep in close touch with the work of the College and attend the committee meetings.

The new House Committee Chairman, Mrs Jan Bateson, was married to a tuior at Corpus Christi, Oxford, and keenly interested in education in general and Denman in particular. Living as she did at Brill, near Aylesbury, she could run over to Marcham once a week and was available to chair courses when needed.

Thanks to the incentive scheme, money was soon flowing into the Denman Fund once again. The plans for an extension to The Croft had already been passed and the committee now felt they could afford to go ahead with the work. Ambitious plans had also been made for improving the estate, including the clearing of part of the Warren and the replanting of trees. This was a project dear to Dora Tomkinson's heart, but in the end, because of the high cost, it had to be shelved indefinitely. As for the kitchen garden, to everyone's disappointment it was proving an expensive liability, instead of a profitable asset as had been expected. The trouble was it was not really large enough to be what is nowadays known as "a viable unit", taking into consideration the high cost of labour. As for the original idea that gardening students should do some of the labour, in practice this was quite impractical. The conclusion was sad, but had to be faced; it would be a lot cheaper for the College to buy its vegetables than grow them. Accordingly both kitchen garden and glasshouses were let to a market gardener, an arrangement that has continued ever since.

CHAPTER XII

More Expansion

That summer W.I. members who visited the South Bank Exhibition during the Festival of Britain were delighted to find that the centre-piece of the countryside pavilion was a large mural of village life featuring all the different activities of the Women's Institutes, with busy little figures (flatteringly young and pretty, and wearing real nylon stockings) working away at different crafts.

This mural had been designed by Constance Howard, Principal of a London Art College, and had been made with the co-operation of W.I. handicraft experts who had contributed Lilliputian examples of craft work – baskets, gloves, embroidered fish, etc. – which had been appliquéd on to the design.

The work had been commissioned by the Festival Committee and so was the property of the Government. When the Festival closed down it was removed to a place of safety and there it stayed until the summer of 1952 when, prompted by a word or two in the right quarter, H.M. Government agreed that it should be given to Denman College.

Transport presented a problem. An extra large lorry had to be hired to convey the big wooden crate to Marcham and when it arrived at the gates of Denman it was too wide to pass through so a crane had to be brought to hoist it over the top. Removed from its frame by Blackwell, to get it into the house, then re-framed, it was finally hung in the lecture room where it occupies the whole of one wall.

By the autumn of 1952 the transformation of the R.A.F. huts into lecture rooms and kitchens was complete and once again there was an opening ceremony at Denman. This time it was performed by the Rt. Hon. Florence Horsburgh, M.P., the Minister for Education.

Now at last the College had the use of two well-equipped

The first Denman College Sub-Committee, L. to R. Miss Tennant, Dame Frances Farrer, Lady Denman, Lady Albemarle, Miss Tomkinson, Mrs. Neville-Smith, Lady Brunner

Marcham House as it appeared in 1947   *Photograph by J.R.V. Johnson*

The opening
of the College
in 1948;
Sir Richard Livingstone
cuts the ribbon
By courtesy of
Planet News Limited

The grounds of the College contain many fine trees. This is the Weymouth Pine

The Drawing Room

Betty Christmas, the first Warden of the College

Part of the
long herbaceous
border

An embroidery class in progress

A young student on a course for mothers and daughters
By courtesy of Farmer's Weekly

The Country Wife
Mural which was
designed and
made by
Constance Howard
for the
Festival of Britain
in 1951,
and now hangs
in the
Livingstone Room
*By courtesy of
Hulton Press
Limited*

A course on theatrical design

Archæology for beginners - another course during a week for mothers and daughters
By courtesy of Farmer's Weekly

Carving in stone

Learning about stage lighting

Music making

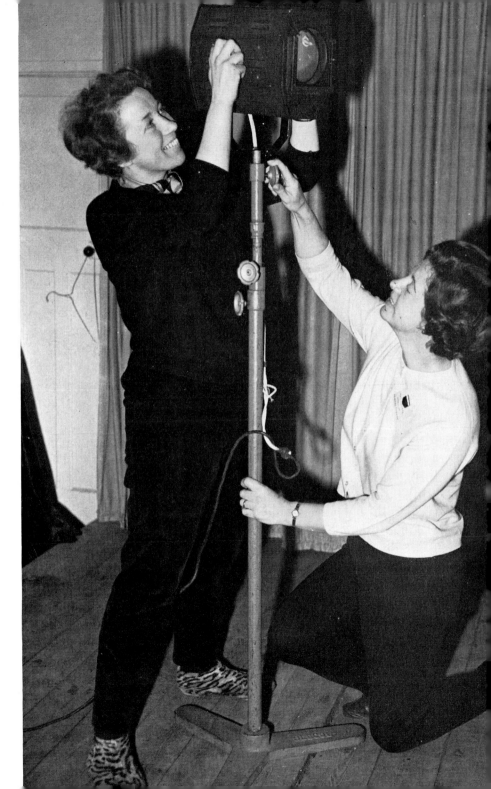

One of the College bedrooms

The hall

The staircase leading out of the hall

The new teaching block including the Bawden Workshop

The new residential block and staff quarters known as Brunner House

The lake in the College grounds

kitchens for cookery and canning classes, by arrangement with the Berkshire County Council, and a room for drama and handicraft demonstrations as well. A flat had also been built into the scheme so that Miss Cumming could live on the premises.

It was not long after this that the New Croft was completed, thanks to a very generous donation from Miss Elsie Corbett, given anonymously. It was a half-timbered building, consisting of eighteen single bedrooms and a number of bathrooms. This time there was no official opening, which was just as well, for the month was February and half the staff were down with 'flu. County and island federations had provided the soft furnishings for the bedrooms and designed the colour schemes. As with the other bedrooms in the house and the Old Croft there were many exquisite examples of handicrafts to charm the students who slept there.

These extra rooms were welcomed by the staff and meant that lecturers could be put up in the College. In the past there had been times when members of the staff had had to give up their own rooms because of pressure on accommodation and take their bedding to the summer house or to the linen cupboard, according to the time of the year.

The original aim of being able to accommodate fifty students comfortably, with single rooms for those who disliked sharing had now been accomplished, and no further expansion was planned for the time being.

"These extra rooms," the Warden wrote in *Home and Country*, "will mean that approximately 400 more students a year can stay at the College and this should add an appreciable sum to the income of the College. It should mean too, that members from the same institute will stand a better chance of coming together."

To mark the beginning of the new Elizabethan Age a course on Elizabethan England was held, soon after the opening of the New Croft. It was a "B" course intended for W.I. speakers with some knowledge of English history who would be willing and able to give talks afterwards on the subject to W.Is in their counties. The idea was something of an experiment, for no one knew the sort of demand there might be for such speakers.

"There were about twenty of us", wrote a young student from

Leicestershire, who had been asked to do a report on the course, "alongside a Folk Dancing school, of whom we saw but little. On the whole we were verging on the elderly and assured. When called to present our credentials in front of the others I felt for a few minutes that I should not be there . . . Mrs Yeo was our chairman and was marvellous. Our tutors were young, too, and this I appreciated very much . . . Dr Butler, the chief tutor, a young man of colossal intellect, was pleased with us; I was enthralled by him. . . ."

With the extra lecture room and craft room at "Home Acres" it was now possible to run courses in pottery. Blackwell, who was consulted about how to obtain a potter's wheel, had a look at one in use at Cheltenham College and made a similar one himself. Soon pottery and clay modelling courses were attracting students of all ages.

Painting had always been the Cinderella of the arts amongst the institutes, and up to this time there had been no courses in oil painting. For some time the Education Committee had hesitated to include any practical courses in the graphic arts, believing that there would be little or no demand. However, their views had been changed after an art appreciation course during which the young woman art teacher had suddenly announced: "Now I'm going to *make* them draw!" and to everyone's surprise, including the students themselves, did just that.

So drawing and sketching courses began to appear in the programme and later, painting in oils was included too, largely due to the enthusiasm and encouragement of Mrs Bawden, who as well as being married to an artist was herself an authority on design in art.

It was also through Charlotte Bawden, together with "Duffy" Rothenstein (now Mrs Eric Ayers) who had recently begun teaching art at Denman, that the College was able to show the work of a number of important contemporary artists, who were persuaded to allow some of their pictures to be exhibited at the College for periods of six months. John Aldridge, Prunella Clough, Edward Bawden and Michael Rothenstein were amongst those who co-operated.

This scheme came into operation in 1953 largely as a result of the success of the painting courses, the students having said how much they would welcome the chance to see and study contemporary paintings, for few had the opportunity to go to exhibitions when at home.

Here it should be said that as a member of the Denman House Committee and later as one of its education advisers, Charlotte Bawden played an invaluable part in widening the College's horizon in the field of art and design, finding the best possible tutors and lecturers for courses on these subjects, and being always ready to give talks, or take the chair herself.

During the summer of 1953 a working party of fourteen W.I members came to stay in the College for two weeks to make new curtains and chair covers for the hall, which was beginning to look somewhat shabby after five years' wear and tear. They also helped the staff in the tricky job of fixing up lighting equipment for the stage at Home Acres and making the stage curtains. By the time they had finished all was spick and span for Denman's fifth birthday party.

Before the party there was a tree planting ceremony to mark the occasion. Sir Richard Livingstone, who had been invited as the guest of honour, planted a cut-leaf beech and Elizabeth Brunner an oak tree. Both have flourished and are now quite sizeable trees.

Speeches and compliments followed the ceremony. Lady Brunner described Sir Richard as the ideal choice for their guest of honour and Sir Richard, in response, said that he had always regarded Denman College as in many ways the most inspiring of all the post-war adult colleges.

"Since I have retired," he continued, "I have done a good deal of travelling . . . and I always urge my audiences to come and see Denman College when they are in England and, on their return home, to go and do likewise. . . ."

The birthday celebrations were followed, shortly afterwards, by a stock-taking conference. A survey of the past five years had been prepared by the Warden; in general it presented an encouraging picture. Fifty per cent of the institutes had had one or more members attend a course; the number of courses had doubled since 1948 and the College could now draw on a panel of really good speakers. A scheme for training teachers in various crafts was also proving very successful.

The popular courses, such as Floral Arrangement, Patchwork, Dress-making and Home Decoration were usually over-subscribed;

but some of the others were proving hard to fill. The least successful had been on Local Government and social problems.

One of the questions discussed at the conference was whether the College should run week-end courses from time to time to cater for members who had jobs and could not, therefore, come during the week-time. The difficulty here was that this could only be done by sacrificing some of the staff's free time. However, it was finally decided to include one Friday to Sunday course in the following year's programme as an experiment.

Another more controversial question was whether to continue the policy of joint sessions. Plenty of students had been critical of these, but the conference still felt they were of value in bringing students together and should be retained in some more acceptable form.

It was decided, therefore, to hold one joint session on the first evening, when the Warden would welcome all the students together and describe each course and its purpose, after which they would split up into their separate groups; and on the last evening they would all be together again for an entertainment of one sort or another. Those who had never been to Denman before would still be taken on a tour of the College and grounds by the Warden, but this tour would now be optional.

This decision, while something of a retreat from the original policy of combining the practical and cultural in every course, was a commonsense compromise based on experience and has worked well ever since.

CHAPTER XIII

Years of Change and Farewells

At the end of that summer Monica Sims resigned in order to take a job at the B.B.C. and a new tutor was appointed. This was Miss Delphine Dickson, an attractive young woman who held a London University degree in history and had also graduated in Sociology at McGill University in Canada. Before coming to Denman she had worked for the World Health Organisation.

By this time Betty Christmas's health was once more causing concern and although she carried on gallantly, by the beginning of the following year she was forced to spend much of her time either in bed, in her cottage in the grounds, (known to everyone as Christmas Cottage) or undergoing treatment in hospital.

It was a difficult and distressing time for the staff. Loyal and devoted, they gave her all possible help and support, going back and forth to her bedside, so that she was kept in touch with all that was going on, yet spared the small day-to-day problems and protected from too many visitors.

They and the committee knew that Denman was her life-line and all were agreed that so long as she was still able to control the College and plan its future there would be no question of anyone else taking over. And so long as she remained at Denman Betty Christmas never gave up, nor admitted to the increasing pain she had to bear, as the disease that was to kill her tightened its grip.

Lady Denman had also been ill for some time with a painful arthritic condition. Shortly before the 1954 A.G.M. she went into hospital for an operation which would, it was hoped, relieve the pain; she knew there was a risk, but preferred to take it rather than "staying alive feeling C3" to use her own words.

The operation took place the day before the A.G.M. At first it seemed that it had been successful, but then her heart suddenly failed and she died on June 2nd.

It was towards the end of the afternoon session at the Albert Hall, when a message from Lady Burrell, Lady Denman's daughter, was brought to the platform with the sad news that her mother had died that morning.

It was a great shock, for everyone had been hoping that she was on the road to recovery. The message was passed around the Executive who sat grief-stricken as the meeting continued. No announcement was made; the message had included a request from Lady Burrell that the news should be withheld from the delegates because she felt that it would not have been her mother's wish that the meeting should end on a note of sadness.

But by the late afternoon the news was in the evening papers, so it was as they made their way home that the delegates learnt with shocked surprise and sorrow that the woman who had led their Movement so wisely for so many years had died on the day of the meeting she had chaired so often.

In the weeks that followed many suggestions for a memorial to Lady Denman came to Headquarters from members. Most wanted it linked with Denman College. One idea much favoured was for a fund to provide bursaries; another for an addition to the College buildings. However, while the Executive were in favour of a memorial linked with the College they felt it would be wise to wait and see how much money came in before deciding on how to spend it.

Lack of reserve capital and shortage of money generally was a continual worry to those responsible for the College. Already they had had to raise the boarding fee to seventeen shillings and sixpence and tuition fees to ten shillings, but expenditure was exceeding revenue by more and more each year, despite an annual grant of £1,000 from the Ministry of Education and an income of around £1,500 from the Endowment Fund; and although it was accepted that the National Federation should make a grant to the College, there were those who felt that the limit had nearly been reached.

In such an economic situation the programme planners could hardly have been blamed if they had played for safety and stuck to well-tried, popular courses with waiting lists, shelving any ideas for subjects likely to have a minority appeal. Besides, there were husbands to be considered too. If, for instance, a member decided she would like to learn dress-making, or improve her skill in pastry making or preserving, her husband was much more likely to agree to look after himself and the family in her absence than if she proposed taking a course in eighteenth-century literature or modern poetry.

Nevertheless, new titles, catering for minority interests continued to appear in the programme each year, and though some were slow to catch on, most justified their inclusion in the long run. Some delighted their sponsors by proving an almost instantaneous success. One of these was a course with the celestial title "For Those Who Play Stringed Instruments".

On a September evening in 1954 eighteen students arrived for this course. Some carried cellos, some violins, some violas. There was even a double bass. They played throughout the morning, broke up into duets and trios, played through the free period in the afternoon, and turned up for chamber music in the evening.

They were all ages, from youthful to white-haired and a bit rusty. And when they finally departed, their arms almost too tired to carry their instruments, they were heard to ask: "But when – *when* may we come back for another course?"

Another experiment was photography, described as a course for those who have cameras and would like to learn how to take better photographs. Betty Christmas, noticing that both Sam, her labrador and Remus, the College cat, were always being snapped by students, had decided that photography must be a hobby of many students, and suggested that a course for those who wanted to improve their technique might be popular.

Her guess proved correct; the course was an instant success and variants have appeared regularly in the programmes ever since. It was taken, like nearly all subsequent courses, by Mr Robert Rose, a professional photographer from Oxford.

On one occasion he decided to take his group of students into the churchyard in Marcham for some practical work on picture composition. In need of a bit of height for the picture he was taking, he scrambled on to a conveniently placed tombstone. A moment later he found to his horror that the whole class was enthusiastically following his example, clambering on to graves or mounting tombstones where they could, each intent on taking the best possible photograph. But the picture that still remains in Mr Rose's memory is of the Vicar's face as, just at that moment he came through the churchyard gate.

In the spring of 1955 Betty Christmas planned an outing for the staff, to celebrate the news that she was to be recommended for an O.B.E.* This, she insisted, was an honour for the College, not a personal one. But when the day came for the outing she was too ill to go. To please her the staff went, sadly, without her.

Soon after this, knowing that she could no longer hope to recover, she sent in her resignation. When she left Denman she went first to stay with Edith Leathart, who had been staying in the cottage looking after her for some weeks. Later she went into a nursing home in Beaconsfield where her many friends visited her regularly, keeping her in touch with all that went on at Denman.

It was while she was in the nursing home that her portrait, which now hangs in the hall at Denman, was painted by "Duffy" Rothenstein (now Mrs Eric Ayers) at the request of the College staff.

The death of Mrs Esther Neville Smith in a car accident that summer was another great loss to Denman. As an intellectual force her influence on the W.I. Movement had been considerable and her enthusiastic support of the idea of a college an important factor in gaining its acceptance by the majority. Since the opening of the College she had been a regular and much valued speaker there. She had the gift of communicating knowledge without a hint of patronage and could quickly infect an audience with her own enthusiasm.

"Talking to her was always delightful," Elizabeth Brunner wrote in an obituary in *Home and Country*. "About making a cake she could become lyrical and I am sure her cakes were delectable and as excellent as her talks on books."

After the Warden's resignation the staff carried on, as they had been accustomed to do, during the many weeks of her illness. Christina Beckton had been looking after the residential side of the College from the start, with the help of Barbara Lilley and knew the job thoroughly. Hard-working and conscientious, she was popular with the staff and students alike; on the other hand she had had little to do with the educational side.

Up to this time she had been known as "College Secretary";

*In the 1956 Honours List Lady Albemarle received the D.B.E. and Lady Worsley-Taylor, for many years a member of the N.F.W.I. Executive, a C.B.E.

72

now she was officially up-graded to Bursar, with responsibility for the general running of the household and estate, whilst the organization of the courses was left to Delphine Dickson, who was academically well qualified for the job, had already proved her ability during her two years at Denman and was also well-liked.

Happily, these two had always got on well together, different though they were in temperament, and when asked by the Executive if they were willing to run the College in double harness until a new Warden was appointed, they agreed to do so. To ease the burden on the educational side Miss Dickson was given an assistant tutor.

That year – 1955 – the College lost the valuable services of Mrs Yeo, who had to resign from the Education Committee because of her husband's ill health. There was also a new chairman of the Denman House Committee, on Mrs Jan Bateson's retirement. This was Miss Margaret Rotherham, a Vice-Chairman of the N.F.W.I. Executive and a Warwickshire member.

At the 1956 A.G.M. Lady Brunner told the meeting that more than £13,000 had been subscribed to the Lady Denman Appeal Fund. Half of this was to be spent on a new dining-room for the College, while the other half would be invested to yield an income for bursaries and for the general upkeep of the College.

This was Elizabeth Brunner's last annual general meeting as Chairman. There was a murmur of dismay from the delegates when her decision to retire was announced; but as Mrs Methuen said: "The burden which falls on the shoulders of the Chairman of the National Federation is no light one. . . ." Indeed it is nowadays practically a full-time job.

The new Chairman was Lady Dyer. Of small build, but wiry, a dynamo of nervous energy, she had already served as Vice-Chairman for several years, so her election was no surprise. It had, in fact, been prophesied by Betty Christmas many years before. After meeting Barbara Dyer at a conference well before she was elected to the Executive she had remarked: "There goes a future Chairman of the National".

Ready though she was for a rest, Elizabeth Brunner felt she must remain on the Executive for one more year to see through to the end of the National Drama Festival which had been planned during her term as Chairman, and in which she was deeply interested.

W.Is could choose to act one of a group of five verse plays by Robert Gittings, which had been specially commissioned for the Festival by the N.F.W.I. Executive and published under the general title of "Out of this Wood". Denman had already run a couple of courses to help producers and actors who intended to compete, and although some members thought the plays a bit too highbrow, the challenge was taken up by hundreds of institutes and led to performances of remarkably high standard. The finals were held in a West End theatre in the presence of H.M. the Queen Mother, who presented the awards.

CHAPTER XIV

The Widening Gap, and Other Problems

For more than two years Denman had no official Warden. The programme of courses went out to the institutes as usual, the mixture much as before, plus a few new subjects. Leatherwork was added to the list of handicrafts taught; there was a course on "Writing a Village History" for the local historian, and for the first time a course on Science.

While the final responsibility for the choice of courses rested (until 1957) on the Education Committee, from time to time the views of the members were canvassed at county conferences, on the planning of Denman programmes; so that in general the subjects chosen were based on the wishes of the majority, although room was always left for some minority interests and experiments.

The Science course appeared in the programme not too alarmingly as "Science and Ordinary People". However, as it was a "B" Course, the students, sponsored by their County Federations, could be regarded as rather more than ordinary members.

Through the good offices of some of Denman's Oxbridge contacts, an eminent team of lecturers had been booked: Sir Raymond Priestley on the peaceful uses of atomic energy, Sir George Allen on electricity and Dame Kathleen Lonsdale on chemistry; all leading authorities in their particular fields.

To some of the students the prospect was a bit daunting. Would they really be able to follow these learned lecturers, let alone carry back anything coherent to fellow members in their counties? Wouldn't their lack of scientific education be embarrassingly obvious?

Such fears were quickly dispelled once the course got under way. There was to be no struggling with formulas; there wasn't a bunsen burner in sight. The science taught was basic; it dealt with the forces and resources of daily life and much to their relief the twenty-seven guinea pigs found the lectures by no means beyond their capacity to follow. Better still, they enjoyed themselves, for not only were Dame Kathleen, Sir Raymond and Sir George instructive and enlightening, they were also lively and entertaining, as the best speakers are. As for Sir George, he was even encouraging about the future, foreseeing a world in which people would live comfortably, warmly and healthily, thanks to peacefully harnessed nuclear power – if they had enough sense.

Before the course ended these science students met to discuss how to carry the message back to their counties, for this had been the main purpose of the exercise. Ideas put forward ranged from one-day inter-county schools to competitions and quizzes in the W.I. for the painless assimilation of scientific knowledge.

Back in their counties many of them set about organizing conferences, with some success. But it was to be several years before "A" courses on science subjects, however basic and utilitarian, became an established feature of the programme. That they did in the end was largely due to the persistence of Mrs Pat Jacob, who chaired the first "B" course, and later became Hon. Treasurer of the National Federation. Possessed of a keen and logical mind, and having herself had some scientific training, she argued that in this present age Science had its place in the Denman programme in the same way as the arts had. It was the old question of the two cultures.

She won her point in the end, but for a start "A" science courses were kept on a practical level. They had titles such as "Science the Housewife's Friend. . . ." and were to do with things like nylons, plastics and refrigerators. Probably it was optimistic to include four of these courses in one year, and certainly there was no rush to fill the places. But although at least one course had to be cancelled Mrs Jacob refused to be discouraged, maintaining it was Denman's job to stimulate demand. In the end she was justified by the acceptance of Science as part of Denman's educational programme.

One result of running the first science course (a similar "B" course was held later) was that the N.F.W.I. was made an honorary corporate member of the British Association for the Advancement of Science and four W.I. members were able to attend the annual meeting at Sheffield that year, Pat Jacob being one of them.

In November 1956 death ended the cruel illness that Betty Christmas had fought so bravely for five years.

"Never once during those long weeks and months did she complain. She kept her interest in the doings and welfare of Denman College right to the end. She will be remembered amongst those who in a short time accomplished a long time. I don't suppose anyone will know what it cost her to resign from Denman".

These words were spoken by the Rev. I. M. Haines, Vicar of Marcham at the memorial service held in Marcham Parish Church on November 9th. In a tribute in *Home and Country* Dame Frances Farrer, General Secretary of the N.F.W.I. wrote:

"Blessed indeed is the Federation to have been served by someone of such rare qualities of mind and spirit. Though she has gone from us now, surely these qualities will live on at the College and will remain an enduring inspiration to all who had the privilege of knowing and loving her."

During 1956 some 1,900 students came to Denman and, as usual, there were disappointed applicants for the most popular courses. On the other hand, some courses had to be withdrawn because of lack of support, and others – "The Problems of Old Age" was one – failed to attract more than a few students. That year Mrs Parker, cook-caterer since the College first opened, resigned and was replaced somewhat unsuccessfully. On the bright side, an anonymous donor generously paid for the library to be redecorated and the House Committee made it known that there would be one or two places reserved for members who would like to spend a peaceful few days at Denman reading and studying in the library without having to attend a course. This was possible because it was seldom that all the students' beds were in use; a situation unknown at the present time.

Headed by the Bursar and Tutor as acting wardens, the staff worked loyally and often short-handedly to carry on the tradition established by Betty Christmas; but the lack of one person in overall control to co-ordinate the work of the College and plan ahead, inevitably brought about a general running down.

In retrospect it may seem odd that so long a time was allowed to elapse before the appointment of a new Warden; the difficulty was that, to those who had known and worked with Betty Christmas, she was irreplaceable. As long as she was living and still taking an active interest in Denman, to appoint her successor seemed out of the question. After her death, because of her close relationship with the staff the Executive felt it would be wise to wait a while, and with two senior members of the staff able to keep things going, there seemed no need to make the appointment in a hurry. Better, they thought, to take plenty of time to find the right person.

In the meantime it was decided to appoint a Denman College Committee to be responsible for both the domestic and educational affairs of the College, instead of dividing the responsibility between a House Committee and the Education Committee, as in the past. This was not only a better arrangement from the administrative point of view, but gave the new committee far more scope to plan future policy.

Elizabeth Brunner, Charlotte Bawden, Margaret Rotherham and Sylvia Gray, all of whom had been members of the House Committee, continued to serve, the last named being elected Chairman.* Two newcomers were Dr Enid Browne and the Marchioness of Anglesey.

At thirty-three Shirley Anglesey was the youngest member of the N.F.W.I. Executive. The daughter of two well-known writers – Charles Morgan and Hilda Vaughan – she was keenly interested in Denman and was to become the next Chairman.

Once formed the new committee brought in extra brain power by co-opting Mrs Margery Fisher, a graduate of Somerville College, Oxford, an author and critic and an authority on children's books. This was a shrewd move, for Mrs Fisher, a W.I. member of many years' standing, has given invaluable service to the College ever since, advising on literary courses, contacting lecturers and herself taking courses on writing for children and some of those on local history and literature. She has also written a revised version of the Denman College Souvenir Booklet.

Miss Briant, who represented the Board of Education (as it was then called) on the N.F.W.I. Executive, was also invited to join the committee and gave a good deal of help on the educational side. A year later Mrs Ing, an Oxford don and a good friend of the College

*Miss Gray resigned from the chairmanship the following year when she was elected N.F.W.I. Hon. Treasurer. In 1969 she became Chairman of the National Federation.

since its foundation as well as a regular lecturer, agreed to be co-opted to advise on educational policy. Mrs Fisher and Mrs Ing were, in fact, Denman's first "educational advisors" although not officially described as such at the time.

Amongst the many problems which faced the new committee the most worrying was the ever-widening gap between expenditure and income. Although expenses had risen steeply since 1948 the boarding fees had only been increased once, by a mere half crown; in the same period inflation had reduced the value of the Endowment Fund. But the real trouble was that the College was not being run on an economic basis; for far too many days in the year bedrooms were empty and no money was coming in.

By the end of 1956 the accounts showed an excess of expenditure over income of well over £3,000, some £500 more than the previous year. As usual the difference was made up by a grant from national funds, but Mrs Methuen, the Hon. Treasurer, was becoming concerned at the increasing charge on N.F.W.I. funds, themselves under pressure owing to the rise in the cost of living.

Lecturers were now costing more, occasionally as much as fifteen guineas a lecture, although there were many who generously cut their usual fee, or waived it altogether. So, reluctantly, the boarding fee was raised to £1 per night (which included all meals) and the tuition fees went up as well, rising to thirty-five shillings for specialized whole week courses, such as pottery and clay modelling.

There is no evidence that these increases were resented, or caused any students to cancel; certainly no one wrote to *Home and Country* to protest. In fact the increases were well overdue and at £4 10s for four days full board plus first-rate tuition, a course at Denman was remarkably good value.

CHAPTER XV

The New Warden

At about the time when the N.F.W.I. Executive were beginning to look around seriously for a Warden, someone suggested to Cecily McCall that she should apply for the post. Since she had resigned from her job as Education Organizer in order to contest a parliamentary seat in the 1945 General Election, she had done various kinds of social work and was, at this time, working for the National Health Service in Norfolk. She had also written a book on the W.Is for the Britain in Pictures series.

After some hesitation, for it meant giving up her cottage in Norfolk and a pensionable job, she applied for the Wardenship and was appointed. In the meantime Delphine Dickson had resigned from her job as Tutor. After four years she was, as she afterwards admitted, exhausted and badly in need of a rest. However, she did stay on until shortly before the new Warden took over.

Cecily McCall took up her appointment in August. Almost at once she began to introduce changes. Like the proverbial new broom she was eager to sweep away all the cobwebs. She believed that the College had become inward-looking, and that change was being resisted for the sake of "keeping things as they always have been". Her first job, as she saw it, was to "let in the light". She then wanted to widen the whole range of courses so that the College became a spearhead for the further education of women.

Four weeks after her arrival a paragraph in *Home and Country* announced that institute outings to Denman would be welcome on any afternoon of the year (bar Sundays and the Christmas holiday period) instead of being restricted to two weeks during the summer when the College was closed for students.

Institutes that had been waiting their turn for two or three years (sometimes very resentfully) were delighted by this news and bookings poured in. Unfortunately the change created serious administrative problems for the staff and some inconveniences for students, who were not too pleased at being disturbed if they happened to be resting on their beds in one of the rooms included in the tour. Hordes of members tramping through the rooms made extra work for the domestic staff, especially in wet weather, and at the end of the tour the visitors had to be served the inevitable "cuppa". But Cecily McCall argued that if they saw the College in operation they would be far more likely to book for a course.

She also argued that if visitors arrived without an appointment, as they did from time to time, they should still be welcomed and shown around. This was after she discovered a party of American sociologists being refused admittance. They had, they said, been on their way to Windsor, but had decided they would rather see "a live College than an ancient monument" and came to Marcham instead. So she showed them around personally. She also decreed that if W.I. members staying in the neighbourhood wanted to see the College they should be allowed to do so.

In fairness to the staff it should be said that the appointments rule had been made to protect Betty Christmas when her health was beginning to fail, and later retained because no one had time to cope with unexpected visitors.

The handsome new sound-proofed dining room, designed by Lionel Brett, and built with part of the Lady Denman Memorial Fund, was completed a few weeks after the new Warden's arrival, and officially opened in October by Lady Denman's daughter. The cherry-wood tables and mahogany chairs came from the Elizabeth Christmas Memorial Fund.

The installation of a dish-washing machine put an end to the students' washing-up rota – to the regret of some, including head-housemaid Phyllis Gosling who had enjoyed getting to know the students as they shared with her the homely task of drying dishes.

After the dining-room had been paid for the £7,500 left in the Fund was divided equally between the College Endowment Fund and the Bursary Fund.

Now that there was more dining space the idea of admitting day students cropped up once again. When it had been considered in the past, one of the objections put forward (apart from lack of space) had been that the College was essentially a residential one and students who only attended study sessions (like day pupils at a boarding school) would not be sharing fully in the community life.

On the other hand, it was argued that if there were members of neighbouring institutes who for one reason or another couldn't be away from home for a night, but wanted to take a course it would be sensible to let them fill up courses that were only partly subscribed, and helpful to College finances to collect some more tuition fees. And although day students wouldn't be paying full residential charges, they would be paying for their meals.

The Warden was warmly in favour of the idea and it was decided to give it a trial. As a result quite a few Berkshire and Oxfordshire members enrolled as "day students" who might otherwise never have come to the College.

By this time a new Tutor had been appointed in place of Delphine Dickson. Miss Geraldine Wirgman, a willing, likeable girl, came to Denman straight from Oxford and was soon hard at work helping to get out the new programme of courses. For some years past these had been running at around 115 a year, now the number shot up to 180, with courses every other week-end and no closing down for Bank Holidays. Amongst the new titles for 1958 were two that reflected the Warden's particular interest in sociology (she had at one time worked in a Borstal institution) – "Planning a New Town", a week-end course, and "The Farm Worker and His Family . . . his life, his job and his Wife's Kitchen".

But perhaps the most striking innovation in the 1958 programme was the invitation to mothers to bring their babies or toddlers to Denman for a week in May, and to families to come with their children to a Family Week in August. The mothers were offered a choice of three courses: "Looking your Best" (which included dress-making sessions), "Drama for Actors" and, for the academically minded, "Travel from Coaching Days to Comet". Trained nurses would look after the babies during the study sessions and sitters would be provided for the evenings.

For Family Week in August the choice of courses: Pottery, Puppetry or the History of the Cotswold Country, with expeditions to beauty spots and places of particular interest. Children, who had to be over eleven and under fifteen, would camp in the grounds under supervision.

Both ideas – the nursery for students' babies and the invitation to husbands and older children to come to Denman during the summer holidays–had been considered before, but had never got further than the discussion stage. Seeing them as a new and exciting way of widening the scope of the College, Cecily McCall carried them through.

Not surprisingly she encountered some opposition. The senior members of the staff were shattered at the thought of screaming babies in the College, and all the extra work and bother involved when everyone was already so busy. Fifteen cots had to be begged or borrowed from somewhere, a couple of trained nurses engaged and local W.I. members recruited to help.

Then the B.B.C. asked if they could film the enterprise, a request that couldn't be refused (and was, of course, useful publicity) but resulted in even more confusion. There were problems over nursery food, not to mention nursery washing, and complaints were expected from students taking other courses when they were awoken at dawn by the wailing of a baby next door.

However, despite these anxieties and forebodings, when the dreaded week came and seventeen W.I. mothers arrived with eighteen babies, all the fuss and upheaval suddenly seemed worthwhile. The babies and toddlers quickly captivated the staff (one of the chief objectors spent much of her spare time playing with them) and it was rewarding to see the mothers so blissfully relaxed and happy in their brief freedom from domestic cares. Most of them had travelled long distances; one came from Cumberland, another from Norfolk. A thoughtful husband had read about the course in *Home and Country* and applied on behalf of his wife so that she should have a much needed holiday.

The week did produce some problems and put an extra strain on the staff, but when it ended all the mothers were insistent that it should be repeated. One of them summed it up as "a three-fold gain – combining a break from the routine of household chores and the endless supervision of small children, expert tuition, and the opportunity to make friends with women of the same age and interests."

Between the Mothers and Babies Week and the arrival of husbands, wives and children in August for Family Week, Denman put on its first public Flower Show.

"We want more members to come to the College and more

would come if they knew what it was like. So it is going to be open to all members and to the general public on July 6th and 7th this year, when there will be a Flower Arrangement Exhibition and Competition . . ." Cecily McCall wrote in *Home and Country*. County Federations were urged to enter floral arrangements (a challenge that most took up) and no limit was put on the number of tickets sold.

The result was hundreds of coaches pouring into Marcham for the two days of the Show bringing some 4,000 W.I. members.

Some flowers came from as far away as Jersey, and a doctor drove his wife and son up from Cornwall, saying the journey was well worthwhile. Large numbers of local people took the opportunity to have a look at Denman too. It was all rather like a gigantic garden party with the usual English garden party weather – grey skies and drizzle. Still, as the College had been transformed into a bower of flowers this hardly mattered.

Constance Spry, who came to present the awards was complimentary about the arrangements, noting approvingly that they were in good taste with "nothing skewbald", and made the competitors feel virtuous as well as talented by telling them that they were helping the nurserymen and market gardeners.

Successful though it had been, the addition of such a major event to all the other responsibilities of the staff and committee was a strain for all concerned and the idea has not been repeated.

Family Week did not attract as many parents as had been hoped, but twenty-five boys and girls camped rather damply in the grounds and for the first time for many years the gardens rang with the shouts and laughter of children. They cooked their own meals on an open fire, punted on the lake, made friends with Blackwell and Kinchin and were allowed to accompany their parents on some of the expeditions included in the courses. They were, however, kept out of the College itself, as far as possible, so that their parents could pursue their own interests undisturbed.

At the end of the summer Christina Beckton left to take up an appointment as County Secretary of the Buckinghamshire W.I. Federation. She had not been happy working under the new regime and sad though she was to leave Denman she thought it best to resign.

Another idea for bringing in money introduced that summer

was the selling of sets of colour slides of Denman, commissioned by the Warden to help the College funds.

A new Bursar, Mrs Millar, a former W.A.A.F. officer was appointed, but soon it was clear she was failing to hit it off with the Warden. There were other resignations and threats of resignation. Miss Messer, the housekeeper, decided it was time to retire. The cook-caterer left and was replaced by a German cook on the recommendation of Mrs Millar. But soon she too began to talk of leaving. On top of this there was trouble with some of the daily kitchen staff.

In the end, Mrs Drischmann, later to be known affectionately by hundreds of students as "Cookie", decided to stay and was a popular member of the staff for many years, but by then the College Committee had become seriously worried by the staff situation.

As the year drew to a close those mostly concerned with the running of the College had begun to feel that despite Miss McCall's undoubted abilities, energy and drive she was not the Warden they wanted for Denman. They were grateful for what she had done, but felt she had tried to do too much too quickly. The priorities were to fill the College, to establish a permanent staff and to improve its financial position by careful budgeting and costing.

The decision that there should be a change of Warden was eventually taken by the National Executive. Believing that she was being treated unjustly Miss McCall at first rejected a request for her resignation. The Executive, however, felt unable to alter their decision and she left early in December. Miss Wirgman also resigned in sympathy, but agreed to stay on until her successor was appointed.

It was an unhappy episode. Distressed as they were at the way things had turned out, the National Executive and the Denman College Committee believed that the decision had been the right one and that subsequent events have proved this, although when the dust had died down there were some misgivings about the way in which it had been carried out.

It was not easy to succeed Betty Christmas and it is never easy to be an innovator. Certainly Denman must always be grateful to Cecily McCall for some of the new and stimulating ideas she introduced, in particular the Mothers and Babies and the Family Courses which have since become an integral and most worthwhile part of the College programme.

CHAPTER XVI

Holding the Fort

Now that Denman was once again without a Warden no time was lost in advertising the appointment, meanwhile the College closed down as usual for the three-week Christmas recess.

This time there was no question of the existing administrative staff being able to carry on unaided. Neither the Bursar nor the Tutor had the necessary experience; in any case Geraldine Wirgman had already declared her intention of leaving. Of the original residential staff only Barbara Lilley remained and she was nearing retirement and had all the work she could handle.

Disappointingly, the advertisement that appeared in *The Times* brought little response, and those candidates who did apply were all quite unsuitable. Faced with the prospect of having to cancel courses and remain closed until the right person could be found, the Committee turned in desperation to Mrs Lesley Ferguson.

Lesley Ferguson was just the sort of person people turned to when hard pressed. She was the widow of a clergyman, had served with the W.A.A.F. during the war and been awarded the O.B.E. At the age of sixty she decided to fulfil an old ambition and take up flying as a hobby. Before the year was out she had gained her pilot's certificate. At the same time she was working as part-time General Organizer for the N.F.W.I., a job which brought her many friends in the Movement.

Since her retirement she had been living not far from Marcham with her two daughters, so she was more or less on the spot when the N.F.W.I. Executive asked her if she would take charge of the College as a stop-gap measure, until a new Warden could be appointed.

Although well into her sixties and no longer robust she agreed to come to the rescue; but the work was more exhausting than she had realized and while she carried on valiantly, by the end of March she felt she was coming to the end of her tether and reluctantly told the committee that she would not be able to continue after April.

So once again an emergency meeting was called and this time it did seem that the College might have to close temporarily. Everyone had already racked their brains to think of someone else who could be relied upon to hold the fort and one name *had* been suggested – a past chairman of the committee who was an ideal person for the job. But she was on a visit to the States.

Nevertheless an S.O.S. went out to Mrs Jan Bateson begging her to return to England and take over from Mrs Ferguson as "temporary, part-time warden".

Jan Bateson had been off the committee for a couple of years, but she had kept in touch with the College, knew the staff and was familiar with the routine. Her family were grown up, her husband was working in Oxford all day and her home, at Brill, was near enough for her to travel to Denman daily. If it was a question of putting in a few hours a day on a temporary basis she decided that she could probably manage it. So, not without some misgivings, she agreed to step into the breach from mid-April.

Everyone was delighted and felt that no better choice could have been made. Not only was Jan Bateson extremely capable, but she had the gift of getting on with people. Hurrying back to England she took over from Mrs Ferguson as arranged.

She was soon to find that her "part-time" day at Denman could well start at 8.00 a.m. and continue till eight at night, although she usually managed to get away around 6.00 p.m. Apart from the routine work of ensuring that fifty or more students were fed, instructed and made to feel happy and at home in the best Denman tradition, there were all sorts of unexpected jobs, such as having to take charge of a day nursery full of toddlers while the professional nurse was off duty.

Then, to add to her problems, the staff situation became even worse. The Tutor, Geraldine Wirgman, who had postponed her departure for several months, left in May and at the end of June the Bursar also resigned. With no likely applicants in sight for either of these posts there was nothing to do but distribute the work amongst the remaining staff. Fortunately a capable young woman, Peg McWilliam, who had been giving part-time help with the secretarial work, was willing to act as temporary full-time Tutor, but it was not until September that a new Bursar was appointed.

However, by this time Mrs Bateson did at least know that her responsibility would end that autumn, for during the Easter holidays a suitable candidate for the Wardenship had applied and would be taking over in October.

Meanwhile, the wheels were kept turning somehow, with the loyal support of Miss Lilley, who knew everything there was to know about Denman, and with "Cookie" a tower of strength in the kitchen. College Chairmen, too, were invaluable during those difficult months, taking over when Jan Bateson went wearily home in the evening. This meant that they were left in complete charge until after breakfast the next morning, with responsibility for the smooth functioning of the College and the well-being of its sixty or so occupants.

Those willing to accept this responsibility (volunteers had been appealed for) were given a briefing by Lady Dyer, the N.F.W.I. Chairman, who made it plain that the job was no sinecure. As one of them recalls: "We were told that this was *not* a rest cure; neither were we to 'swan' it around the College being in authority and contributing nothing."

Strenuous though the task proved to be, the volunteer chairmen found it a rewarding and stimulating experience, and happily no one had to cope with any major disasters.

The 1959 programme, planned during Cecily McCall's wardenship, included no less than three separate Mothers and Babies' Weeks, as well as a Family Week at the end of July. Inevitably these caused more administrative headaches. There were also more experimental courses than usual; an Astronomy Course, with Patrick Moore of B.B.C. fame as a lecturer (husbands were invited to come and stargaze with their wives), a full week's course on "South Africa, from the Boer War to Apartheid", a week-end course for husbands and wives on "The Daily Press – Who controls it, Edits it, Writes for it", and "Problems of Race", a course which dealt with such tricky matters as mixed marriages and integration.

As well as being slow to book, courses of this type put extra strain on the staff, since no one knew quite how they would work out.

Also there was apt to be difficulty in finding suitable lecturers, which added to the office work.

Still, at least it was a fine summer, long and hot, and Mrs Bateson was grateful for it. In fact the only wet spell was when the boys and girls were camping in the grounds during Family Week. But as it wore on, with every day as full as the one before she began to despair of ever getting down to the work of putting together the 1960 programme which should have been completed by the end of May.

In the end it was her husband, F. W. Bateson, a tutor at Corpus Christi College (now a Fellow) and friend and mentor to countless undergraduates, who came to the rescue in the best tradition of W.I. husbands. When the College closed for the first week of September they moved in to the empty house together and made up the complicated jig-saw of suggested courses and conferences into a final programme.

As a break from helping on the academic side Mr Bateson also put in a stint in the garden, for the much-loved College gardener, Mr Church had died suddenly that summer, leaving Mrs Bateson with yet another problem – to keep the garden in order while trying to find a new gardener.

As it was such a fine summer the National Executive felt they could take a chance on arranging a garden party at Denman for the delegates who were coming to England before attending the triennial Associated Country Women of the World Conference, which was being held in Edinburgh during August. But this was too much to expect of the weather and the party took place indoors, as garden parties in this country usually do.

It was a point of honour for the College to offer overnight hospitality on such occasions, even with a resident staff consisting of only two. So Mrs Bateson moved in again, this time bringing her daughter as another pair of hands, and the English country house tradition of morning tea in bed on Sunday was maintained.

The problem of catering for a collection of guests with a wide variety of customs and creeds (necessitating special food) complicated the week-end even more, but somehow the worst pitfalls were avoided and the party ended in smiles and goodwill all round, and a gratifying comment from the delegate from Sweden, who remarked as she said good-bye: "English hospitality is something for the world to learn".

In September Mrs Bateson thankfully handed over the residential and estate side of the College to Miss D. Collett, the newly appointed Bursar, who had already had several years' experience of bursarial work. Before coming to Denman she had worked in a residential establishment for handicapped children. The set-up at the College struck her as wholly amateur, but none the less agreeable. At the time of writing she is still Denman's Bursar and has seen the annual turnover doubled.

The new Warden, Miss Marjorie Moller, M.A., was also a professional. She had been headmistress of Headington School for Girls in Oxford for twenty-five years and, at the age of sixty, was due to retire. As she said later, she felt she had quite a lot of energy left, and as she wanted a change she decided that work connected with adult education would appeal to her.

By a lucky chance a friend mentioned to her that a Warden was wanted for Denman College. Interested she wrote for details and was invited by Dame Frances Farrer to meet the Committee. She had already been to Marcham to have a look at the College by that time, and when she was offered the appointment she gladly accepted it.

CHAPTER XVII

A New Appeal

The W.I. was an entirely new sphere for Miss Moller. She had been a professional teacher all her life and, until she took up her appointment as Warden of Denman, she had had practically no contact with the Movement. To ease the transition Mrs Bateson stayed on for the first two weeks before going off for a well-earned rest, confident that now all would be well.

The new Warden's standards were extremely high, as the staff were quick to realize. Little went on that escaped her observant gaze. She had the authority one would expect in a woman who had been headmistress of a large school for many years, tempered by a good-humoured smile and a quick sense of humour.

Although there was still an immense amount of goodwill for the College on all sides, money was uncomfortably short. For the first time since 1948 the number of students showed a decrease on the previous year. Courses were losing money through insufficient applicants and quite a few were having to be cancelled.

Shortage of staff made it very difficult to run Denman efficiently, yet the committee felt they could not increase outgoings by taking on extra staff. Meanwhile continuing inflation had reduced the value of the Endowment Fund and other investments. It could be said that for some time the pace had been too fast and the College had already been showing signs of having outgrown its strength.

Because of some disquiet over the ever-increasing grant from the N.F.W.I. General Funds the National Executive decided to have a debate on Denman's finances at the autumn Consultative Council.

As Chairman of the Denman College Committee, Shirley Anglesey opened the debate, explaining the position and the dilemma that faced her committee. In 1959 the grant from General Funds had been nearly £4,500, and this sort of help really could not continue without cutting down on other activities and throwing the Movement out of balance, which no one wanted. Yet to raise the accommodation charges to a more realistic amount would be to put the College out of range of members with small incomes and make the granting of bursaries too much of a burden to small institutes. She was asking, therefore, for some constructive suggestions.

This put the ball in the county representatives' court. Rising to the occasion they were unanimous that Denman *must* continue and must keep its standards high. No one thought that students should have to pay the economic cost of staying in the College, but there was a general feeling that they could be asked to pay a little more; say another two shillings and sixpence a night, with husbands, since they were not members, paying an extra five shillings.

This still left the greater part of the gap to be bridged, and once again there was only one answer. The institutes must be asked to help.

No one enjoyed the prospect of another appeal, but it was nearly six years since the original Denman College Fund had been closed and in the interval another 500 institutes had been formed (bringing the total to around 8,400) and these had never been asked to contribute. In the circumstances a new appeal did not seem unreasonable.

So, when the 1960 programme went out, the new charges went up to 22s 6d a night for W.I. students and 27s 6d for husbands – still a remarkable bargain compared with the charges at most educational establishments. Amongst the 159 courses offered, six catered for mothers with babies (the babies were now limited to a dozen at a time) and two weeks in August were once again set aside for family courses.

With an N.F.W.I. art exhibition announced for 1963, the programme shows the upsurge of interest in painting and the visual arts, offering as it does six practical painting courses and seven on various forms of art and art appreciation. Nevertheless, Drama still leads with ten courses, three more than Embroidery, the most popular of the handicraft courses. An entirely new venture was a course on contemporary Russia.

Confident now of support from the county federations for a new Denman College Appeal, Barbara Dyer and her Executive Committee decided to call 1960 "Denman College Year", and launch an Appeal Fund at the Albert Hall during the A.G.M. Their aim was two-fold; to raise at least £25,000 and to encourage more members to make use of the College.

When she stood up to launch the Appeal on the second day of the meeting, Shirley Anglesey, looking as always cool and collected, put the matter succinctly; expenses at Denman had been rising steeply and it was now necessary for the institutes to help with some financial support, if they wanted its unique work to continue. The Fund would be open until the end of June 1961, but she asked for promises of the amounts institutes and individuals hoped to contribute, before the end of October.

The next step was to mount a publicity campaign, and immediately after the A.G.M. every institute received a personal letter from Lady Dyer asking for a contribution, explaining why the money was needed and how it would be spent; for as well as increasing the Endowment Fund in order to provide a bigger income, some much needed improvements were planned, such as the installation of oil-fired central heating.

To make doubly sure that the message went over, the county federations were invited to send a representative to a conference at the College in July, from which, it was hoped, they would return home and publicise the campaign amongst their fellow members. A film about Denman was also made by a producer of independent documentary films, Mr Harvey Harrison, who was also a W.I. husband and whose wife wrote the script. This was hired out to institutes for several years until it finally wore out. Colour slides were also taken and sold in large quantities.

While the campaign to secure the College's future went ahead, the new Warden was getting to know the members, not only as students at Denman, but up and down the country through the talks she gave at county meetings.

At the end of her first year she summed up her impressions in an article in *Home and Country*. Her first had been of a gay and friendly atmosphere, a mixture of liveliness and kindness that made newcomers quickly relax and feel at home; a second impression, amazement "that so much work could be achieved in such short courses", especially when many students were complete beginners in the subjects they came to study.

Although she herself had been a science teacher, she was equally interested in the humanities and was anxious to do all she could to help those with little formal education to a better understanding of the arts; for plenty of Denman students did (and still do) fall into this category.

The determination of Denman students in general to acquire knowledge or technique was always a surprise and a delight to lecturers and tutors and one of the reasons why there were few who were not ready to return, once they had taught at a course or given a lecture. As "Duffy" Ayers put it, when describing the way her painting students worked: "It's as if they had only these four days to live!", but then, for many students, their four days at Denman has only been achieved through long-term planning, complicated family arrangements and probably a last-minute intensive cooking session, so as to leave husband and children a well stocked larder. After so much effort it is natural that every minute at Denman is precious.

By the end of 1960 everyone was feeling much happier about the College's future. An anonymous donor had given the Fund a splendid start with a cheque for £3,000, many individual members had taken out seven-year covenants, and – with six months still to go – the Fund had reached more than £18,000. At the College itself the new Warden had settled into her job and was on excellent terms with the College Committee, then under the able chairmanship of Mrs Kathleen Bullows, who was a great help to Denman at this time.

So it seemed that at last the corner had been turned. Nevertheless, although Miss Moller found the job of running Denman interesting and rewarding it was also proving harder work than she had expected, for the staff was still under strength. If the College was to run smoothly it meant there was little time off for anyone.

During the years following Betty Christmas's resignation staff shortages and changes had bedevilled the running of Denman, putting far too heavy a burden on the faithful few. While the number of students rose year by year the residential staff establishment had hardly changed, and in practice was often less than in 1948; for instance, most of the time since Miss Messer's resignation there had been no resident housekeeper. On the domestic side it was not too difficult to recruit good daily help from Marcham; but secretarial help was another matter. Shorthand typists from Abingdon came and went from year to year, usually with gaps in between.

It was sad when, in 1961, two members of the original staff, Barbara Lilley and William Blackwell, both reached retirement age.

Miss Lilley, the first Warden's Secretary and a devoted friend of Betty Christmas had worked unsparingly for the College for thirteen years; Blackwell, handiest and most helpful of handymen was also going to be greatly missed. Both still visit Denman and Blackwell, who was given fishing tackle as a farewell present, regularly fishes in the lake.

Before the end of 1960 Peg McWilliam left and was replaced for a short time by temporary help, but there was a gap of some weeks before Miss Hilda Jones was appointed in January 1961 with the title of "Studies Secretary", later to be changed to "Director of Studies".

Energetic and full of go, she had enlisted in the W.R.N.S. at the outbreak of war, after taking a degree in English Literature at London University. During her fifteen years in the Service as an Accountant Officer she played both squash and tennis for the W.R.N.S. and was for a time stationed in Australia and Northern Ireland.

Between leaving the W.R.N.S. and coming to Denman she had worked for six years at Barnett Hill House, the British Red Cross Society's College in Surrey, where she had become an Assistant Commandant. Interested as she was in adult education, with the same belief in its importance that had inspired the early W.I. pioneers, the Denman appointment had immediately appealed to her for its wide scope and range of interests.

Not long after Miss Jones took up her appointment Mrs Nora Lewis, who had recently become a widow, came to Denman on a Soft Furnishing course. She was looking for a job and it had occurred to her that there might be something she could do within the W.I. Movement. She mentioned this idea to one of the staff who suggested that she should see the Warden. Although a bit doubtful as to whether she would be able to do anything useful at Denman, for apart from having been president of her W.I. she had no special qualifications, she took the advice, had a talk with Miss Moller and was offered the post of housekeeper.

As the Warden had been quick to see, Mrs Lewis was just the person for the job. A woman of sympathy and understanding, with an excellent sense of humour, she was soon thoroughly enjoying life at Denman, hard work though it was. Under her régime all the blankets were washed at the College once a year, instead of being sent to the laundry, and the worn-out linen was slowly replaced, much of it by students, who would be encouraged to give pillow slips or sheets if they proposed a "thank-you" gift at the end of a course.

Miss Moller was insistent that however great the pressure of work the friendly, club-like atmosphere of the College should be preserved. The staff were expected to be available each morning between breakfast and the first study session, and again when all the students foregathered in the hall for their mid-morning coffee break, in order to give help or information, or a word or two of reassurance if needed.

It was on one of these occasions, during a week-end course for husbands and wives, that an elderly woman turned suddenly to Mrs Lewis and gasped: "Do you see that man over there, with white hair? He proposed to me when I was eighteen and I've never met him since!"

Later this student made herself known to her one-time suitor and his wife and soon all three were great friends.

According to Nora Lewis, who enjoyed observing human nature at Denman, W.I. husbands usually fell into one of three categories. There were the "good W.I. husbands", cheerful and good-humoured, always ready to lend a hand if needed. One even organized the morning tea rota. Then there were the pressed men, wary and not quite at ease, who would usually relax a bit after the first few hours and finish up admitting that they were enjoying themselves after all. And finally there were the reluctant husbands, deeply suspicious of the whole exercise and obviously wondering why they had ever become involved.

Such a one was the gentleman who walked about with his head bowed and his hands clasped behind his back for the first three days, speaking to no one until, by a happy chance, he found some plants flowering on a patch of ground by a stream in the warren, recently cleared by Mrs Lewis. This discovery not only cheered him but loosened his tongue. He was, it then emerged, an authority on bog plants and for the rest of the course he chatted about his discovery to anyone willing to listen.

Another reluctant husband declared that the only reason he had come was because his wife had presented him with the acceptance form for both of them as his birthday present!

On a different occasion two husbands who had come with their wives on a Nature Course were overheard talking together at breakfast. "Did you tell them at the office what you were doing this week-end?" asked one. "No fear" said the other. "Coming to a women's college would have been bad enough – but *bird* watching would have been too much!"

Many of the men who have been at Denman for the first time have expressed their surprise at the high standard of lectures. "I wondered what I was doing sitting listening to an American talking about our villages," remarked one husband who had come with his wife on a local history course, "but my goodness, she's brilliant!"

From the beginning Denman had gone out of its way to welcome foreign visitors. During Betty Christmas's wardenship members of Canadian W.Is whom she had met on her tour often turned up to renew their acquaintance and learn about the British W.I. College. Students from Commonwealth countries frequently attended courses, interested groups from overseas studying adult education come for the day, members of overseas women's organizations have been entertained for a night or a week-end. But until the 1960's none had ever come from the other side of the Iron Curtain.

Determined to achieve a break-through in the interests of peaceful co-operation, the National Federation invited two women from the U.S.S.R. to spend three weeks in England as the guests of the W.I. during the early summer of 1961. This invitation was accepted and in due course Madame Burkatskaya from the Ukraine, a Deputy of the Supreme Soviet and Madame Maslova, a teacher of English at Moscow University, arrived at Heathrow.*

Both turned out to be friendly, likeable women with a great sense of fun. Madame Burkaskaya, stout, round-faced and in her forties; Madame Maslova tall, good-looking and in her twenties. For most of their visit they stayed in the homes of W.I. members, while

---

*Since this time members of women's organizations in Czechoslovakia and Poland have been entertained at the College and the Russians have paid a second visit.

good-will built up on both sides. Finally they came to Denman and the slight apprehension that had preceded their visit melted like snow in summer. They stayed for several days, saw several courses in progress, tried their hand at canning fruit and made friends all round.

Before they returned to Russia they attended the National Federation A.G.M. at the Albert Hall where, amongst other things, they heard Lady Anglesey report that the Denman College Appeal Fund had reached £35,000 – £10,000 more than the minimum target – and would be kept open until the end of September that year.

Of this sum £30,000 had been given by the institutes (with outstanding contributions from Jersey, the Isle of Man and Merioneth Federations) and the rest had come from individuals, various firms kindly disposed to the W.Is and from trust funds and legacies.

Then she went on to tell the meeting of the success of Denman College Year's other aim; to make the College better known amongst the institutes. Already the greater publicity had resulted in a record number of students applying for courses, and the demand for the film of the College and the colour slides had been beyond all expectations.

Four months later when the Appeal officially closed the total amount subscribed was £39,243. This meant that when all the money from the many seven-year covenants came in the hoped for £40,000 would have been comfortably exceeded.

It was certainly a splendid result, tremendously encouraging to the Denman Committee and the staff and to all the members up and down the country who had worked and schemed to put over the Appeal.

Now, for the first time, the College had adequate reserves against future capital expenditure and the sort of eventualities that are bound to crop up in the maintenance of an estate of the size of Denman; at the same time it was possible to increase the Endowment Fund to provide a badly needed additional income.

CHAPTER XVIII

Reorganization and Recovery

After the crises of the late fifties the early sixties was a period of steady recovery. Apart from a pair of cottages built on the estate to make it easier to recruit outdoor staff, there was to be no further building for some years.

As the number of students taking courses climbed to over three thousand a year, so the gap between income and expenditure narrowed; at the same time the reorganization of the office work on more efficient lines resulted in fewer cancelled or poorly filled courses. These had been a drain on resources for many years and the saving was considerable.

Week-end courses were held more often and between 1960 and 1962 the number of courses open to husbands trebled. The choice, too, was wide. They could study literature, art, music, archaeology or architecture; enjoy the pleasures of the countryside, try their hand at making wooden toys or home decoration, learn about car maintenance, or how to grow better roses; make their own wine, or prepare for retirement. By which time the assiduous Denman husband might reasonably expect to find himself well equipped to fill the remainder of his days.

A keen collector herself, Miss Moller introduced week-end courses on such subjects as Victorian jewellery, porcelain and china and old silver. These quickly became a popular choice for married couples, but husbands were also allowed to opt for different courses from their wives, so long as they were there together. This quite often happens; indeed some husbands have become regulars and try one course after another. One, married to a committee member who had been going to Denman to "chair" courses fairly often, finally decided that he had better have a look at this place she was always disappearing to, and, though without much enthusiasm, agreed to attend a course on the Norman Conquest.

Pleased as she was that he had decided to take the plunge, his wife was not altogether sure that he would be happy, and when he hardly left her side for the first twenty-four hours she began to think his visit would be a complete failure. But happily the Denman charm worked, and by the second day he was obviously enjoying himself. Since then he has been accompanying her willingly once or twice every year.

Occasionally the separate choices of a husband and wife are unexpected. One veteran husband, having attended eight lecture courses, decided to make his ninth "Advanced Cookery", while his wife was learning how to do interior decorating and be handy about the house.

The generous response to the Denman College Appeal Fund had been a great morale booster to staff and committee alike, and at the end of 1961, with the number of students up by 600 and the budget balanced, everyone could feel that recovery was assured.

Early in 1962 a wellwisher, who preferred to remain anonymous, presented the College with £10,000, asking that the greater part be invested in a Benefaction Fund, the income from which should be used "for the furtherance of the general educational purposes of the College". This munificent gift, showing as it did great faith in the future of the College, was a tremendous encouragement to everyone concerned. Naturally there was great speculation as to the identity of the donor, but this has never been divulged.

Five years later some of the money was to be used for the Benefaction Bursaries Awards, of which more later. Meantime outworn educational equipment was replaced and some new and badly needed teaching aids bought.

An interesting development at about this time was the series of social history courses devoted to several well-defined periods – "The Elizabethan Age", "The Age of Craftsmanship – 1680–1730", "The Regency Period" and so on. Each course was designed to show the student the arts and crafts, architecture and costumes of the period by means of lectures, colour slides, visits to museums and typical buildings. Husbands were welcomed to attend as well.

It was an ambitious idea and its success owed much to the hard work and enthusiasm of Charlotte Bawden and Helena Hayward. As an expert on English furniture and the decorative arts, and a well-known writer on these subjects, Mrs Hayward had been a regular lecturer at Denman for some time and became one of the College's educational advisers during Miss Moller's wardenship. Her recruitment to the committee forged a new link with the Victoria and Albert Museum, as well as with the British Museum and London University, since she was working in close touch with all three (as she still is) and was thus in a position to put the College in contact with suitable lecturers – always a tremendous advantage when it comes to planning courses.

After she had been at Denman for a year or two Miss Moller decided that one or two changes were advisable. Although the Mother and Babies courses were very much appreciated by the dozen or so mothers who attended them, they did take a lot of organizing, occupied a great deal of room (since the babies had to have a playroom) and were rather a strain on the staff. So it was decided to reduce the number to one week during the summer and instead include a special week for mothers and daughters. Daughters had to be between fifteen and twenty and could either share a room with their mothers or with some of the other daughters. The courses offered were all practical ones – such as dress-making, flower arrangement, clay modelling, and so on. This idea quickly took on and mothers and daughters courses have featured in the programme ever since. Having once broken the ice by coming to Denman with their mother the daughters often return on their own or with a friend.

One girl who came with her mother struck up a friendship with another W.I. daughter and after corresponding for a couple of years they met once again on a Drama course. The mother, an Essex member, first went to Denman to learn carving in wood and stone, has returned many times to try other courses and has now become expert in theatrical design. "One should go to Denman to learn something new", is her view.

On a damp November afternoon in 1962 a bust of Sir Richard Livingstone was unveiled in the garden at Denman by his old friend Sir John Christie, the Principal of Jesus College, Oxford, before a gathering of relatives and old friends. Not long before his death at the age of 81 in 1961 Sir Richard had sat for the sculptress Kathleen Parbury; since then she and his family had felt that they would like the bust to stand in a place with which he had special association and their choice had fallen on Denman.

Life size, it stands against the north side of the house, showing Sir Richard with head thrown back, in the characteristic pose he so often adopted when lecturing.

Some little while before Elizabeth Brunner, who had always been a great admirer of Sir Richard, had suggested the Mural Room, where lectures were held, should be known as the Livingstone Room, as a permanent tribute to his memory. It was, by this time, somewhat shabby after years of wear, so as a gift to the College in Sir Richard's memory, it was refurnished and redecorated by a small group of members in time for the unveiling ceremony.

There was now a new chairman of the National Federation, Mrs Gabrielle Pike, who had been the first president of Marcham W.I. when it had been re-formed in 1948. The wife of the head-master of a well-known boys' prep. school, her warm and gay personality, genuine love of people combined with good looks and a flair for dress not only made her a popular choice amongst the institutes, but did much to persuade the Press that the tweedy image of the W.I. was out of date. To have such an old friend and good neighbour as Chairman of the National Federation was naturally a great source of satisfaction to Denman and there was much rejoicing amongst the members of Marcham W.I., several of whom were on the College staff.

Because of the amount of work involved in welcoming W.I. outings to Denman, and the cleaning up afterwards in bad weather, the all-the-year-round invitation was modified during Miss Moller's time to "come between March and November". This arrangement still holds good and usually results in around 3,000 members seeing the College and grounds annually.

Miss Moller also came to the conclusion that the boys' and girls' camp during Family Week was not really worth all the trouble. Invariably it had coincided with the worst summer weather, and what with tents collapsing and clothes having to be dried out, it seemed far better to allow students' families to sleep in the College and attend the courses with their parents, provided they were over eleven and under fifteen.

The Sewing Week-end was another bright idea of hers which

has won a regular place in the programme. Busy housewives, who want a break from chores and the family, but don't like being idle, can come to a week-end course bringing the sort of sewing that can be done on their laps, and at the same time be mentally refreshed by music and readings while they work.

During the early sixties, while the number of students was steadily increasing, set against the total membership of the institutes (by this time nearly half a million), the proportion of members who had taken a course was still small, and there were institutes that had never even had one member at Denman. In general, it could be said that half the students attending in any one year had been at least once before. Satisfactory though it was when students returned over and over again, if Denman was to stay in business in the long run it had to have a continuing flow of new blood.

How best to put the idea over to the ordinary member was an old problem. Publicity helped and bursary schemes overcame the problem of expense. Special awards, such as the bursaries won by magazine secretaries who pushed up the sales of *Home and Country*, often brought in members who would never have thought of applying for a course. One magazine bursary winner from the Channel Islands was thrilled to travel by train for the first time in her life when she made the journey to Denman. But there were still those who, for one reason or another, felt that Denman was not for them; for the diffident, particularly, the idea of going to stay in a college amongst strangers and of perhaps appearing stupid or inadequate was altogether too alarming, however much they wanted to learn a craft or attend a lecture course.

As a former headmistress of a girls' boarding school Marjorie Moller had known plenty of shy and homesick girls and could appreciate this problem. Her idea of overcoming it was to introduce the County Course. This was an arrangement by which county federations could take over all or part of the College and run a course for a group of their own members, who would naturally mostly be known to each other.

At first there were some difficulties in making this scheme work, but County Courses have now become part of the programme and do serve as a very useful introduction to Denman for students who would otherwise never find the courage to come on their own.

Amongst the hundreds of students who come to Denman some, inevitably, are eccentrics. Experienced chairmen learn not to be surprised by odd behaviour. "My dear, I snore!" confided one elderly lady to the chairman of her particular course, "but just turn me over on my side. I shan't wake." After which she settled down happily in bed wearing a man's cap adorned with a red feather.

On another course one student arrived without luggage looking remarkably bulky. Asked by a member of the staff if she had a suitcase she replied cheerfully: "Oh, I never bother with luggage. When I travel I wear all the clothes I'm likely to need."

Occasionally very shy students are overcome with nerves on their arrival, like the young woman who was persuaded by a friend to come on a painting course. On her first evening she lost courage completely, and sat terrified in her bedroom insisting that she wouldn't be able to compete; that she would pack at once and go. After much argument she was finally persuaded to change her mind and turned out to be far the most gifted student on that course.

As well as the eccentric and the shy there are, sometimes, unhappy women who have come to Denman to escape from themselves, or from some situation or problem. A chairman of a lecture course, noticing a middle-aged woman looking strained and obviously unhappy asked if she could help in any way but was rebuffed rather shortly. However, as the course continued this student did seem more relaxed and showed increasing interest up to the end of the course, when she came to the chairman, apologised for her earlier brusqueness and told her story. Not long before she had been in a serious motor accident in which a close relative had been killed. She was president of her W.I. and thinking it might help her the members had persuaded her to apply for a course at Denman. Unwillingly she had done so, to please them. Now she knew they had been right; through Denman she had "turned the corner".

Courses at Denman are not intended to be rest cures and sometimes four or five days intensive study is rather more than elderly or frail students have bargained for; yet drop-outs are rare, and in the excitement and satisfaction of acquiring a skill or learning something new amongst a group of like-minded people, aches and pains are forgotten. One woman on a gardening course acknowledged that she was turned ninety, but she finished the course with the rest. Quite a few students are physically handicapped; some of these have become skilled craftswomen; others have gone on to further studies at their local technical colleges.

Chairmen are sometimes puzzled as to why on earth a certain student ever applied; as for example the young woman who after a couple of days told her chairman she would have to leave. She really couldn't stand it, she explained, the place was far too full of women!

Then there are the crafty, like the Essex member who went on a painting course, but took with her a half-knitted pullover reckoning – correctly as it turned out – that she would be sure to find someone at Denman who would finish off a bit of knitting at the neck for her. This same student, when asked what she thought of the College replied tersely: "The cleanest place I've ever been in!"

Not having understood the rule that all gifts must first go before the committee, students sometimes bring an offering with them. One woman, it was noticed always carried around a large paper parcel. Despite discreet questions from the staff she clung to it determinedly throughout the course, refusing to disclose its contents. Finally her moment came and overcoming her shyness she presented the Warden with a large, china piggy bank, made by her husband who was a professional potter. This is now used for donations to College funds.

As well as looking after the students on their course, chairmen are also responsible for seeing that the lecturer is on time for each session – a task which sometimes means rousing reluctant risers, or searching for the "absent-minded professor" who wanders off during the afternoon, forgetting his after-tea session. Over the years the College has built up a reputation for cossetting its lecturers and it is rare indeed for anyone to refuse to come a second time.

CHAPTER XIX

Enter Miss Dolphin

After five years as Warden Miss Moller resigned in the summer of 1964, on reaching the age of sixty-five. She had come to Denman at a time when it seemed that the College was heading for disaster; under her firm direction it had been brought back on course and was once again sailing in calm waters. During her term as Warden the number of students attending courses had risen by nearly sixty per cent and by the time she retired the annual account was showing a profit for the first time.

"By the retirement of Miss Moller Denman loses an outstanding Warden," Mrs Elizabeth Harris, then Chairman of the Denman Committee, wrote in *Home and Country*. "She brought to the College wide experience and great organizing ability, and it must be a source of pride to her that the College has an assured place in the education world."

On the educational side her knowledge of people in academic and teaching circles, and her own high standards, had a considerable influence on the enrichment of the programme. When ideas for adventurous courses came up at committee meetings she was always ready to support them, although it must be said that such courses did not always catch on right away. But Miss Moller had faith, and in the long run her persistence was justified.

The new Warden, Miss Ann Dolphin, had already been appointed and took over as soon as Miss Moller left. When she was first interviewed for the post Denman was little more than a name to her, as she admitted later, so she decided she had better attend a course, as an ordinary student, before taking up her appointment, choosing a verse and prose speaking course. This was an experience she later found invaluable.

Tall, dark-haired, with a quick, perceptive intelligence and a warm interest in people as individuals, there was something about

Ann Dolphin that recalled Denman's first warden. From the very beginning she made a point of attending some part of each study session on the first evening of new courses; she also found time somehow to make contact with every student before their stay came to an end.

She was just under forty when she was appointed Warden. A graduate of St Hilda's College, Oxford, and of the London School of Economics, her first job had been as a social worker amongst munition workers during the last year of the war. Ten years as a Child Care Officer followed, then four years of travel, working her way round the world in a variety of jobs, including a spell on a New Zealand sheep and cattle ranch. Her last assignment, before taking up the Denman appointment, had been as Organizing Caterer to the Guildford Cathedral refectory. During this period she had joined Churt W.I.

When asked if working at Denman was not rather like living on a main line railway station she agreed that in some ways it was; there were the same tantalisingly brief encounters, the greetings and farewells; but the analogy did not allow for the "regulars", the students who came over and over again, for it was they, as much as anyone, who gave the College its stability and continuity and who were largely responsible for the unique Denman atmosphere – that stimulating mixture of enthusiasm, hard work, friendliness and courtesy.

Each week had a distinctive feel, often a distinctive smell – grease-paint, turps, toffee, the hot dry smell of the kiln when there was a pottery course. And with the ever-changing students there was the ever-changing talk; the jargon of archaeology mingling with the technicalities of carburettors and clay modelling, photography and philosophy; the fascination of meeting the lecturers and tutors, often household names in their particular sphere.

Then there were the days when she went out into the counties – long days, driving to distant and often unfamiliar parts of England and Wales to speak at meetings and conferences and tell the members who had not yet come to Denman all about it; a public relations job this, and one at which Ann Dolphin was notably successful.

Unlike her predecessor, when she came to Denman she found

a well-established, experienced staff. There could have been problems here, but happily there were none.

In the autumn of 1964 Denman experimented with the idea of running three related courses concurrently, with one or two joint sessions, so that each group of students could learn something of the other subjects along with the one they had themselves opted for.

This idea had been suggested by Miss Jones, the Director of Studies, who believed that education at Denman should sometimes be allowed to overlap – instead of always being divided up into neat little parcels.

The three courses chosen for the experiment were all concerned with literature: "The Modern Novel", "Modern Poetry" and "Biography and Autobiography". The lecturers – an impressive team – included Richard Church, poet, novelist and autobiographer, Ruth Pitter, winner of the Hawthornden Prize for poetry, and Janet Dunbar, author of several biographies.

To the delight of those who had supported it, this experiment in "cross pollination" worked out splendidly. The three groups of students mingled enthusiastically and with mutual benefit, and animated discussions went on into the night, the lecturers finding it all as stimulating as their students.

Since then there have been linked courses in modern architecture, modern painting and modern sculpture; in pottery and painting, and the contemporary novel and contemporary drama.

One of the newer trends that had begun to make itself felt during Miss Moller's wardenship and which gained strength in Miss Dolphin's time, was the increasing demand for courses in creative writing.

This had been a somewhat neglected field. From time to time the early programmes would offer a course on play-writing (mainly to encourage members to write one-act plays for the W.I. market – always short of suitable material) but as far as the would-be writer of fiction was concerned that was about all, though courses for W.I. Press Correspondents were regularly held.

The situation soon improved after Margery Fisher joined the committee, and with her help and advice two new kinds of writing courses were introduced; specialized courses in writing for children, and general, mixed courses in journalism, fiction and writing for radio. For advice on this last-named market Denman was fortunate (and still is) in being able to turn to Lorna Moore, Head of the B.B.C. Talks Department, who joined the committee in 1965 as an education adviser and B.B.C. contact.

Since these courses first began to be held several students have had work published, and Mrs Fisher has had the pleasure of reviewing three books for children written by former students of hers. She feels that there is a real need for a follow-up with this type of course in particular, and probably for some others. Some students do form unofficial groups, correspond and criticize each other's work and sometimes meet, but as yet they have no direct link with the College. Perhaps this is something that could be developed in the future?

Up to this time courses on the arts had tended to deal either with a definite period, or the works of one particular writer or composer. Now it was suggested that a study in depth on one particular work might be included in the programme from time to time. Benjamin Britten's "War Requiem" was the first to be chosen for this experiment, the course being a week-end one and open to husbands. As might be imagined the response was fairly moderate, but the experiment is being continued nevertheless.

Another idea tried out during the mid-sixties was the language course. Up till then it had been thought impractical to attempt to teach a language in the short space of a Denman course. However, the popularity of the B.B.C. language courses made it seem worth a try. "Speaking French", advertised as a week-end course for students with some knowledge of the language and open to husbands, was the first to be held. Since then "brush-up" courses in German, Spanish, Italian and French have become a regular feature of the programme; they are linked with the B.B.C. courses and are always well filled – which seems to show that the old idea of the Britisher abroad, trying to make himself understood by shouting ever louder in his own language may need revising.

The introduction of any new subject is bound to be something of a gamble. Since 1964 a system of Course Reports has provided the staff and committee with an instant picture of how every course in the programme has fared. Compiled by Miss Jones, these give all relevant data (including the number of students on the waiting list – sometimes as many as 19) and are an invaluable guide for assessing the value of a course both educationally and from the point of view of cost.

For the College to break even an average of fifteen students per course is needed. But as some of the craft courses have to be limited to a dozen, "lecture courses" are relied upon to even things up by taking twenty-four or, occasionally, up to thirty students. In the same way tuition expenses may vary from fifteen to over sixty guineas, the cheaper course helping to finance the dearer.

CHAPTER XX

Faith Rewarded

Before Miss Moller's retirement the committee had already been warned that the Berkshire County Council would not be renewing their lease of Home Acres when it ran out in 1966. The arrangement had worked very successfully for more than twelve years with Miss Cumming, the R.D.E. instructress and the College staff always on the best of terms. The trouble was that the Horsa huts, which housed the demonstration kitchens and Miss Cumming's flat, were coming to the end of their life, and, after an inspection had shown that they were not worth the cost of repairing the County Council decided that it would suit them best to have their R.D.E. centre in Abingdon.

The verdict on the huts was no great surprise to anyone, for it had been known they would have to be replaced eventually. The question was, should the College be content with providing a demonstration kitchen only, letting students doing practical work use the centre in Abingdon by arrangement with the County Council, as they had used the R.D.E. facilities in Home Acres? Or had the time come when the committee should take its courage in both hands and recommend a comprehensive building scheme to include not only a demonstration kitchen, but a new lecture theatre cum studio, a room for heavy crafts, and more single bedrooms and bathrooms to replace the Old Croft, now not really adequate for modern needs?

As a first step to finding the answer to this very challenging question a small building sub-committee was set up under the chairmanship of Elizabeth Harris, at that time the Chairman of the College Committee. Other members were Elizabeth Brunner, the representative of the Department of Education, Miss McCullough, and the Warden, Director of Studies and Bursar. Later Lady Hemingford, the new College Chairman replaced Mrs Harris and Mrs Bawden became a co-opted member.

III

With two years to go before the lease of Home Acres ran out, no decision had yet been taken when Ann Dolphin was appointed, and she was soon making useful contributions to the general pooling of ideas.

In December 1964, on the eve of the N.F.W.I's Golden Jubilee Year, the County Federation's Denman College representatives (elected annually to liaise between counties and the College) met at Denman for a conference. One result of this was the pleasing idea of planting rose trees in the garden as a jubilee gift from the counties.

Not to be outdone the institutes contributed nearly £70 for hundreds of daffodils to be planted in the grounds to make it an appropriately golden spring.

In the January Honours List for 1965, Elizabeth Brunner received an O.B.E. for her work as Chairman of the Keep Britain Tidy Group. A year later Gabrielle Pike was to be awarded the C.B.E. as Chairman of the National Federation at the time of its fiftieth birthday; these honours for leading W.I. members gave great satisfaction to the institutes throughout the country.

It was an exciting year for W.I. members. The calendar was crammed with celebrations, for as well as a garden party at Buckingham Palace and other national events, the County Federations all marked the occasion with festivities of one sort or another.

As befitted Jubilee Year the 1965 programme was more than usually adventurous. Husbands and wives were invited to go behind the scenes of Weather Reporting and Road Planning; the under-thirty-fives had the chance to bring bright ideas to a course on "The Future of the W.I.", and following a course for parents on keeping in touch with their children, it was a logical step to "An Introduction to Jazz", taken by Avril Dankworth.

Amongst the twenty-one students who took the course on "Outer Space" were three young married women from Kent who, having applied too late to learn cake icing rather dubiously accepted the suggestion that they might like to go to Outer Space instead. In the event, they found the experience thrilling and at least one of them has made a further trip.

In early September Denman held its own Jubilee Garden Party, a colourful affair with saris and vivid African cottons mingling with English summer dresses, and Morris dancing on the green lawns in brilliant sunshine. Once again A.C.W.W. delegates were in England on their way to a Triennial Conference in Dublin and many accepted an invitation to spend the week-end at Denman and celebrate the N.F.W.I's Golden Jubilee. Members of the County Federations' International sub-committees were there to meet them and, of course, the National Executive.

In December Denman said good-bye, with much regret, to Mrs Drischmann who had fed staff and students so well for more than seven years. (She was followed by Miss Elizabeth Channon for three years and then by Miss Jean Maidment, both of whom have kept up the College's tradition of good home cooking.) Up to the end of 1965 Denman had remained "dry". But now that it was coming up to the mature age of eighteen, it seemed a suitable time to apply for a club licence – a decision welcomed by those students who were accustomed to relax with a drink before their evening meal. It also meant that husbands no longer tended to mumble something about getting some cigarettes and disappear in the direction of Marcham around six-thirty, as had been the custom of one or two.

As for television, there are no sets in any of the common rooms, nor are there likely to be. Some of the staff have one and as far as they are concerned the only demand for "the box" is on Saturday afternoons when occasionally an uncontrollable desire to know what won the three-thirty brings an apologetic student to their door.

Before the end of 1965 the building sub-committee, accepting the challenge presented by the necessity of replacing Home Acres, had produced a blueprint for a comprehensive scheme and were already in consultation with Messrs Brett and Pollen, the architects who had designed the new dining-room. Their recommendation that the College should go ahead and start building for the students of the seventies might be called an act of faith since no one knew how the scheme could be financed, apart from launching yet another appeal to the institutes.

And faith was rewarded. Early in 1966, while the plans were still on the drawing-board, Denman received the most munificent gift in its history. This was an anonymous benefaction of £30,000 towards the cost of the new buildings, given to ensure that they should be built to a standard befitting the College.

CHAPTER XXI

Good-bye to Miss Dolphin

Dear Miss Dolphin,

Thank you for all the imaginative thought and hard work put in by you and your staff and the Denman College Committee, which makes Denman such a unique place in which to spend a study course.

Even in the short space of a week-end one is captivated by the atmosphere. . . .

Dear Miss Dolphin,

A wonderful atmosphere at Denman! I learnt a tremendous lot and am now bursting to pass my information on to others. Thank you very much for catering for our creature comforts so well. . . .

Dear Miss Dolphin,

Sincerest thanks for the Benefaction Bursary. I had not realized how much I was in need of such a change. The joy of being able to read during the day with an easy conscience!

Despite my fears to the contrary, my family survived quite well without me, so I look forward to a return visit some day. . . .

Ann Dolphin received many such letters while she was at Denman. During her three years as Warden she always showed a warm regard for human relationships, while at the same time working with a quiet dynamism to bring more students to the College. She had given much time and thought to the planning of the new buildings, and it was sad that she could not be at Denman when they came into use.

Her resignation, because of family obligations, was received with regret by committee, staff and the many students she had come to know.

"Her wide interests and scholarship have broadened the scope of our programmes, introducing many new and adventurous ideas," wrote Lady Hemingford, Chairman of the Denman Committee in a farewell tribute in *Home and Country*. "Her visits to so many counties have encouraged more members than ever to come to the College and her friendly charm has made them feel happy and secure when there. . . ."

Denman lost another popular member of the staff in 1967 when Mrs Nora Lewis came to retirement age. During her six years as resident housekeeper she had been confidante, counsellor and comforter to the worried, the shy and the sick. Anxiety-stricken students, convinced that they had forgotten to turn off the oven, or guilt-ridden because they had deserted their families for four days ("I forgot to make them some custard!" one distraught mother of five had cried) had been reassured by her good sense, and restored to sanity by her sense of humour; the shy were made to feel at home and the occasional cases of sickness were given sympathetic care.

It had been hard work, but as she herself said after her resignation: "It's astonishing how fond of Denman you become – especially when you're away from it."

Miss Dolphin's last year was a notable one in Denman's history; for the first time no course had to be cancelled for lack of support and it was the year that the Benefaction Bursary scheme came into operation.

Financed with the income from the £10,000 anonymous benefaction made to the College in 1962, the twelve bursaries it offered were open to all W.I. members, though with the rider that preference would be given to those who had not already taken a course. Accommodation, tuition and travelling expenses were all covered, and applicants could choose one of eight selected courses, "Outer Space", "The American Civil War and After", the three linked courses on Modern Painting, Modern Architecture and Modern Sculpture, "Planning in Town and Country", "Satire Past and Present" and "Talking Spanish".

As the main purpose of the scheme was to make it easier for the College to run academically adventurous courses none of the craft or other popular subjects were included in the offer.

An equally important aspect was that by offering these bursaries each year the field of potential students was widened, for although the current charge of 32s 6d (£2 for a single room) a night plus a small tuition fee is reasonable enough, travelling expenses can be high, bringing the total cost of attending a course to a sum many hard-pressed housewives either couldn't afford, or wouldn't feel justified in paying in order to study a subject of no practical value, however dearly they would love a few days of intellectual stimulus, and the "joy of being able to read during the day with an easy conscience" as the letter writer quoted previously put it.

The 1968 programme, completed during Ann Dolphin's wardenship and Denman's most ambitious to date, introduced a new series of lecture courses under the heading "The Contemporary World", designed to give students the chance to study the important questions of the day – something many members and their husbands, are anxious to do. Appropriately, since it was Human Rights Year, the first in the series was on "Colour, Race and Creed". Appropriate, too, that one of the lecturers should have been Mrs Sylvia Denman, of the Race Relations Board, who must have felt rather as if she was visiting her family home.

"An Introduction to Philosophy" and "Science and Economics" were two of the new titles; there was "Mediaeval Women" for the history student and amongst the practical subjects one specially designed for the enterprising contemporary Mum, "How to Start a Play Group".

Within a month of this programme going out to the institutes a record number of applications had come in and many courses were already over subscribed.

For several years reading lists have been sent to students some weeks before the date of their course, so that by the time they arrive the ground is already tilled, so to speak, and ready for cultivation – if the student does her home-work conscientiously, as most do.

Lecturers who have been coming to Denman over a period of several years have remarked that students nowadays seem better informed and are more ready to ask questions and take part in discussions. Certainly the wish to learn was there before, but all too often it was inhibited by a lack of confidence and fear of showing ignorance. Silence was safer! But having once broken the ice by coming to Denman with a friend from her own county on a "C" Course, or by taking one of the less intellectually demanding subjects such as "Country Dancing", "Keep Fit", or the ever-popular "Country Housewives", the first-time student meeting "Academics" at meal times and finding them by no means alarming, especially as they are W.I. members like herself, will often decide to try a lecture course next time.

As for the art and craft students, dedicated though so many are to their own special line of country, there are others who love the challenge of new mediums and move from pottery to sculpting in stone; from basketry to lace making and from traditional forms of needlework to the up-to-the-moment techniques in embroidery and design.

The presence of husbands as fellow students has also proved a stimulating influence, putting wives on their mettle and bringing out the male point of view in discussions. Most husbands come to Denman at the week-ends, though retired husbands sometimes join their wives on the mid-week courses. Usually some forty courses a year are open to them, in creative, academic and language subjects, and they average three or four to a course.

CHAPTER XXII

Looking to the Seventies

Miss Helen Andersen, Denman's fifth and present Warden, took over in October 1967. A tall, cheerful woman with a friendly unhurried manner, she had already had some contact with the W.I. as an adjudicator at county music festivals and had stayed in the College when the Townswomen's Guild were there for a week-end during 1965.

Born into a musical family, the youngest of six children, she read both music and modern history at Oxford and was training to be a singer when the war broke out. During the war, while working for the Arts Council (then known as C.E.M.A.) running musical entertainments for civil defence workers, she discovered a talent for administration which was to stand her in good stead some years later when she became Musical Adviser to the Townswomen's Guilds.

After the war she took up her career as a professional singer once more and sang for six seasons at Glyndebourne, in the chorus and as an understudy. Then back to administration again; but the Townswomen's Guild job was part-time so she was able to start and help to run the Cheltenham Opera Group as well.

When she came to Marcham for a week-end, after learning that the post of Warden at Denman was to be hers, it was high summer. The house and gardens were basking in the sunshine, the swans gliding gracefully on the lake, the Friesian cattle grazing peacefully in the water meadows, and the pretty cottage garden belonging to the Warden's house greeted her with a gay show of flowers. For years she had been wanting to get away from London into the country and the prospect of living in such beautiful surroundings delighted her.

Her first impression of the work of the College was of "a wonderfully constructed jig-saw" and of her first week as Warden "one enormous whirl!" Like her predecessors, she was amazed by the variety of courses and greatly impressed both by the enterprise of the students in tackling such stiff and exacting studies, and by the high quality of the lecturers and tutors.

By a happy coincidence there was a course for conductors during her first week. Then the College filled up with the Organization chairmen from the County Federations who came to pool ideas at a week-end conference. No sooner had they departed than she found herself welcoming another cross-section of students – a group of would-be public speakers for a Speakers' School, some experienced needlewomen for an advanced course in Design in Embroidery and some twenty or so students including several husbands whose course was a study of "Satire, Past and Present".

By the time Miss Andersen arrived the final plans for the new buildings had been agreed and the contract was already with a local firm of builders, Messrs Benfield and Loxley. The work was scheduled to start early in 1968 and to be completed in the autumn of 1969 in time for Denman's coming of age*. A ceiling figure of £85,000 for both building and equipment had originally been set by the National Federation but during the inevitable problems and delays in finalising such an ambitious project costs kept on rising and by the end of 1967 it looked as if there was no alternative but to cut out part of the plan and do without the workshop, with its pottery kiln, sinks and so on.

The decision was a hard one to have to take, after all the work and planning that had been done to bring the College up to the standard dreamed of for so long. Then, once again, the situation was saved by another generous donation. Rather than allow any part of the original plan to be sacrificed Sir Felix and Lady Brunner guaranteed the extra money.

In the spring of 1968 the contractors moved on to the site between the house and the New Croft and in April, while students were learning about the splendours of Byzantium, painting in oils, or trying their hand at lettering, the foundations of the new buildings were being laid. Since then staff and students alike have shared in the excitement of seeing them grow.

Mothers and Babies Week, rechristened Nursery Week, was held once again in June 1968, after having been dropped from the programme for three years. This was not due to lack of demand on

* Official opening of the new buildings — April 1970.

the part of the mothers, but because of administrative problems. The 1968 choice of courses during Nursery Week included a newly introduced craft that has recently gained many addicts amongst the institutes – that of Collage.

Another craft taught at Denman for the first time in 1968 was Corn Dollies, a folk art that dates back to time immemorial and until the W.I. became interested was always practised by men. Revived amongst the institutes some ten or so years ago, it is now becoming popular with nimble-fingered members with a gift for imaginative design. The Corn Dolly instructor at Denman, Mrs Stacey Nott, was born and brought up on a farm and is married to an Essex farmer who, as a good W.I. husband, co-operates by growing a patch of the special wheat best suited to make the dollies.

July 1968 saw Marcham cut off by floods when the River Frill burst its banks. At Denman the staff watched apprehensively as the flood water crept steadily towards the house (happily it never quite got there) while three W.I. coach outings, one from Wales, one from the West Country and one from Essex, booked for more than two years to tour the College that day, urged on their drivers to brave the waters, and undeterred by flood warnings and diversion signs, finally made it in the end.

A course on Russian literature held in October, though at first a bit slow to book, drew its full quota of twenty-seven students, greatly to the satisfaction of those who had proposed it for the programme in the belief that W.I. members were ready and able to tackle the Russians. In the event, three students turned out to be Russian speaking.

One who was not, and who had, as she confessed, felt somewhat baffled by the Russian mind after reading the required books in translations described the course as "magnificent". It was, she said, like being back in her Girton days.

The lecturers on this course included Professor Hingley, Oxford University's chief lecturer on Russia and Pasternak's sister, Mrs Lydia Pasternak-Slater, who read her own translations of her brother's poems.

So this story of Denman comes to the present time and the College's twenty-first birthday year. As these words are written the new buildings are rising in a series of hexagonals, their pinky-yellow brickwork in harmony with the mellow stone of the old house; the woodwork and window frames of a finished hardwood that needs no painting.

They stand in a garden area, separated from the house by tall trees. There is a two-storied residential block, with its ten single and two double bedrooms, also a Bursar's flat and accommodation for two other staff. All walls are sound-proofed, wardrobes, chest of drawers and washbasins are built in and there will be wall to wall carpeting. As in the past the County Federations will be responsible for the soft furnishing and will choose their own colour schemes. Those that lose a room with the demolition of the Old Croft are being given priority in the new block.

The teaching block is separate and single storied. It provides a room for crafts, a lecture room equipped for film shows, a studio for drama, painting and dancing (with plenty of storage space for equipment), a workshop to be known as the Bawden room with pottery kiln and sinks, and a preparation kitchen for preparing cookery demonstrations (practical cookery students will go to the Berkshire Tech. in Abingdon).

An unusual and attractive feature of the design are the lantern roofs which top each of the four teaching rooms, giving them an intriguing and slightly oriental appearance, as well as providing maximum daylight.

There is no desire at present to see Denman grow larger, nor for any radical change of policy, which remains faithful to the original conception of a short-stay residential College for W.I. members, offering tuition in a wide range of cultural, creative and practical subjects. Its job, as the present Warden sees it, is to act as a catalyst in the lives of the students, widening the scope of their interests and leading them to study still further; at the same time giving them a taste of community life at its most agreeable.

Students who come as beginners will return to do more advanced work, some, perhaps, will go on to take a teacher's diploma, or continue their studies at their "tech", a place they would have hesitated to venture into if they had not first been to Denman. Amongst the many who come to do creative work there will be a few who will acquire the skill and confidence to become professionals, as some have done in the past.

It could be said that the academic courses are at present little more than appetite whetters for those, admittedly a small minority, who enjoy learning for its own sake or want to study a subject not offered in the curriculum of their local college of further education, or feel they should know more about some contemporary problem. Others come to Denman for the pleasure and intellectual stimulus of hearing first-class lecturers and taking part in discussions – instead of sitting passively before the TV set; and to meet like-minded people. Some may even be schoolgirls, intent on passing their "O" levels, as were a group who came to the course on "The Canterbury Tales".

The programme for the whole year now goes out in August. Every institute receives one copy, with the polite request that it should be made available to the members – a request which, regrettably, is sometimes ignored. However, as a complete list of courses is also published in the September issue of *Home and Country* would-be students can study it there, bearing in mind that those who procrastinate in sending in their application are unlikely to be lucky if they apply for one of the more popular subjects.

By October the Director of Studies is already plotting the outline plan of the next programme on an enormous board, like a giant puzzle, in collaboration with the Warden. To start with she must allow for twenty or so "B" Courses, to comply with the needs of the different N.F.W.I. sub-committees for training future W.I. leaders and instructors. Dates are then fixed for special weeks – "Family", "Mothers and Daughters", "Nursery Week" (now held every other year) and the "County" weeks. After this come the popular subjects asked for by the majority of members, which account for at least 75 per cent of the programme, and which must be included in every year, in many cases with a choice of several dates.

At this point, early in December, the fourteen-woman College Committee arrives (plus the *ex-officio* members) bursting with bright ideas, for the annual two-day programme planning marathon, and the long process of selection and elimination begins. Always there are more new ideas than can possibly be fitted in, however persuasively their sponsors put them forward; always there is the pressure of demand for more of the courses with long waiting lists – painting, dress-making, cake-icing, pottery and so on. But in the end a compromise is reached, not without difficulty, for those who serve on the Denman committee are usually women of independent minds and, dedicated as they are to working for the College's well-being and future progress, ideas can differ on how this is best achieved.

Finalised, the programme will have some 170 courses (of which thirty or so will be academic) and run from the end of the first week in January to the second week in December. There will be at least a dozen painting courses, and about the same number devoted to food; its preparation, decoration and preservation.

There will certainly be six or seven of the ever-popular Country Housewives courses, with places reserved for the first-time students, and about the same number for embroidery of one sort or another. Flower arrangement, pottery, photography, millinery, will all feature at least three times in the programme; so will training for speakers, W.I. officers and committee members.

History, literature and philosophy, science and the law, the management of money, antique collecting, gardening and the study of nature, craft work and creative writing, music and drama, dancing and keeping fit, learning languages and learning how to look one's best; there will be courses under all these headings, and at least two completely new subjects, such as "The History of Printing", in the 1969 programme.

Looking ahead into the seventies there seems to be no reason why more advanced studies shouldn't be offered to those who want to go more deeply into a subject, even perhaps to serve as a preliminary to an external degree course, or linked with the new University of the Air, for which women will certainly be the best customers.

Would there be the demand to justify such an experiment?

Twenty-five years ago the idea that a country housewife would be prepared to go to all the trouble of organizing her family in order to spend four days studying "Archaeology for Beginners", or "Animal Behaviour" would have seemed wildly improbable, yet Denman can now offer these and similar courses confident that enough applications will come in to make running them worthwhile. It can also claim, with justifiable pride, to being the best equipped of the voluntary short-stay Colleges in the country, and that educational circles now regard its four-day lecture courses as the equivalent of a term's course in the average sixth form.

From the beginning the aim has been to provide top quality teaching in all subjects. For craft courses most of the instructors are experts fully or partly employed by the National Federation. Creative courses and those for the various activities (such as dancing and drama), are taken by professionals of known standing. For academic courses the College is able to call on first-class lecturers from Universities such as Oxford, London, Reading, Leeds, Birmingham, Keele, St Andrews and Sussex.

Many of these lecturers have been coming to Denman over a number of years. As well as being authorities on their own subjects they are men and women who delight in teaching and find the responsiveness of Denman students especially rewarding and the atmosphere of the College very much to their taste. Nowadays, active participation in the lecture courses is always part of the syllabus and because the students are mature men and women, coming from many different walks of life, with minds of their own, the question and discussion period, included in each session, can sometimes prove as enlightening to the lecturer as to his class.

There is much to be learned, too, outside the teaching rooms, when students foregather sociably at meal times and after the evening session, or relax in the garden during their free time in the afternoon. Linked by their membership of the Women's Institutes, they start with a common interest, a first step to sympathy and the interchange of ideas; sometimes to a lasting friendship.

Because Denman is first and foremost a place where people come to learn, those concerned in its smooth running (and it runs very smoothly indeed these days) are in favour of co-operation and some participation, but are less enthusiastic about permissiveness. Students who opt out of study sessions in order to sunbathe in the garden, retire to their beds instead of attending the Thursday evening concert, fail to finish their set pieces of craft work, cake-icing, or whatever, or worse still, nip off into Oxford for a shopping spree when everyone else is hard at it, tend not to be regarded with much favour by their fellow students, or their course chairman. Their place, it is thought, would have been better filled by someone who really wanted to do the course. But students such as these are rare birds.

Parallel with the planning of the new buildings, Miss Collett, the Bursar, has been working on equally ambitious plans to beautify the estate and at the same time make it more profitable. The students of the seventies will look across the smooth, green lawns and the lake to a wide sweep of parkland, half-circled by woodlands, growing in value year by year. There will be harmonious groups of poplars, willows and bird cherries, and a woodland ride abloom throughout the spring and summer with dogwood and other ornamental shrubs.

The story of Denman is a continuing one. The students will come and go, men and women, more than three thousand each year; the young, the middle-aged and the elderly, their interests as varied as their backgrounds. They will learn, talk, laugh and make friends, returning home refreshed with new or wider interests. The College is there because they wanted it; it will be there as long as they need it. Its future is in their hands.

INDEX